CHOICES, DECISIONS, & CONSEQUENCES

ALONG LIFE'S JOURNEY

Rudolph Burke

CHOICES, DECISIONS, & CONSEQUENCES

Copyright © 2011 by Rudolph Burke. All rights reserved. Distribution and reproduction are strictly prohibited by law. All Scriptures are from the King James Version, unless otherwise noted. No part of this publication may be reproduced, stored in a retrieval system, or transmitted in any form, or by any means, electronic, mechanical, photocopying, recorded, scanning, or otherwise, except as permitted under Section 107 or 108 of the 1976 United States Copyright Act, without the prior written permission of the publisher or author. Request to the authors should be addressed to **Loyal Leaders Publishing** at publishing@loyalleaders.com

For information about reprints rights, translation, or bulk purchases, please contact: **Loyal Leaders Publishing** at publishing@loyalleaders.com or you can write to Loyal Leaders Publishing, and P.O Box 742, Plymouth, FL 32768.

Choices, Decisions, & Consequences: Along Life's Journey
Author: Rudolph Burke
Cover designed by: Loyal Leaders Consultants
Edited By: Kay Tanner & Deborah Francis
ISBN: 978-0615553535
Published by: Loyal Leaders Publishing. Plymouth, FL

CHOICES, DECISIONS, & CONSEQUENCES

DEDICATED

To my son Michael, Granddaughter Brittney, Grandsons Michael Jr., Ryan, and Malik. Also to the next and future generation may the thoughts in this book inspire you to achieve greatness.

CONTENTS

ACKNOWLEDEMENTS	9
INTRODUCTION	11
MY ANALOGIES OF LIFE'S JOURNEY	17
THE BEGINNING OF LIFE'S JOURNEY	25
TRAVELING THE JOURNEY	27
TO LEAD OR TO FOLLOW	41
TEENAGE YEARS	45
ADULTHOOD	51
RELATIONSHIPS	55
THE FAMILY	63
PARENTING FOR THE JOURNEY	69
THE DIFFERENCE IN THE SEXES	75
WE ARE DIFFERENT BUT EQUAL	81
WHY WE GET MARRIED	93
WHY SOME DON'T STAY MARRIED	99
WHY OTHERS NEVER GET MARRIED	105
HOUSE OF WORSHIP	109
OUR HEALTH	115
DEBT	121
WEALTH	127
RETIREMENT	131
WE SHOULD ENJOY OUR LIFE	139
ABOUT THE AUTHOR	145

CHOICES, DECISIONS, & CONSEQUENCES

AKNOWLEDEMENTS

FIRST AND FOREMOST, I GIVE THANKS TO GOD FOR HIS TIMELY DIVINE INTERVENTION AND INSPIRATION IN WRITING THIS BOOK. THE INTENT OF ALL THE SUBJECTS, ARE TO BRING AN AWARENES OF THE GREAT REWARD WE WILL ACHIEVE WHEN WE PUT OUR FAITH AND TRUST HIM ONLY.

TO PASTOR TONY McCOY AND HIS MINISTRY AT HOPE INTERNATIONAL CHURCH IN GROVELAND, FLORIDA. HIS POSITIVE, MOTIVATIONAL AND SPIRITUAL TEACHING AND PREACHING HAS TRANFORMED MY FOCUS FROM WORLDLY DESIRES TO A PATH OF REPENTANCE AND SALVATION.

THANKS TO MY EDITOR KAY TANNER FOR HER DELIGENT, THOROUGH CRITIQUE AND SCRUTINY OF THE MANUSCRIPT THAT HAS ENHANCED THE GRAMATICAL PRESENTATION.

APPRECIATION TO THE FOLLOWING PEOPLE FOR DEDICATING THEIR TIME AND EFFORT TO REVIEW AND EVALUATE THE SUBJECT MATTERS: RITA SIMON, DEBORAH FRANCIS, GAIL TIMMONS, VALERIE PERSAUD AND OSCAR FRANCIS.

CHOICES, DECISIONS, & CONSEQUENCES

INTRODUCTION

My main reason for writing is to leave a legacy as an accomplished, established and recognized Jamaican author who stimulated, inspired and intrigued the mind of readers to embrace a more spiritual and positive lifestyle. Hopefully, I will be a successful author who will provide a financial and reputable inheritance for my son and grandchildren. I also want to bring a global awareness to the fact that Jamaicans are talented in the field of creative arts on the international stage. Musically, we introduced and established reggae music, which has been recognized and embraced and has brought entertainment and pleasure to music lovers worldwide.

We are also prolific writers that in God's appointed time will be acknowledged prominently on the international writing arena. Since my first book "Journey of Perseverance from Jamaica to America" was published, I became aware of the fact that there were many other Jamaican authors. I am hoping that our writing will inspire and motivate other prospective authors who are waiting in the wings to step out boldly and shine.

As a young man, I had no inclination or desire to be an author because I was not aware that I possessed the gift of penmanship. To be an author in my latter years had to be a divine inspiration from God who motivated me to undertake this venture at this time. He enabled me to formulate and articulate various subject matters, without a college degree or any formal training, in a precise and concise manner for readers to easily comprehend. This serves as a confirmation that we are all destined to fulfill a purpose, but we must be aware of God's presence, recognize his voice and respond to his command promptly, reverently and obediently to realize our hidden talent.

It is never too late in life to realize our full potential and display it in a manner that will be beneficial to others. In the Bible there are two very righteous couples, Abraham and his wife Sarah and Zacharias and his wife Elisabeth who gave birth to their first child beyond their child bearing age. Both their sons had tremendous spiritual influence that impacted the lives of many. This should convince us that regardless of our age or circumstances we should never give up on God in our quest for success, fame and fortune.

With this newly discovered talent I will aggressively pursue a career as an author, dedicated to inspire and motivate readers to elevate their standard of living to the higher spiritual level. As a new author, I find it very rewarding, satisfying and pleasurable when I receive commendation for my first book. "The moving finger writes; and having writ, moves on" (Omar Khayyam). Writing has distracted me from all the negative people and circumstances that are in my sphere and serves as a motivating force for great expectation in the future.

I am hoping that this book will bring an awareness of the many distractions and obstacles that people will encounter along life's journey. Illustrated are the importance of making the right choices which will minimize negative consequences. The intent of the written words is to imprint in the hearts and minds of the readers to stir up their God-given gifts that they are blessed with but are not yet aware of at this time.

Also emphasized is that we should never make emotional decisions, before we distinguish the difference between perception and reality and rationally analyze the situation and then make an objective decision. The consistent theme is never concede to adversity, but be resolute, resilient and perseverant, remembering that nothing that is good ever comes easily. At all times and under all circumstances we should exercise positive thoughts, words and actions with a spiritual walk that will bring positive rewards. If we are convinced that "I have fought the good fight, I have finished my course, I have kept the faith", then we would have executed the winning formula for success.

Our destiny is generally determined by our choice in lifestyle. Chapters are dedicated to the importance of letting go of our past mistakes and disappointment and making the necessary corrections that will enhance our future. The book chronicles our behavior, attitude, problems and solution from childbirth through our senior years. All aspects of our decision making process are covered, including our finances, our health, why we get married, why we divorce, church fellowship, retirement, and how best to enjoy our life.

I hope that after reading this book, it will enlighten, inspire and be a motivating tool that will enable the reader to be elevated to a higher level where prosperity resides. We should always remember that God wants us to have life in abundance, and we should not settle for anything less.

I authored my first book titled **Journey of Perseverance from Jamaica to America** that was published in May, 2010. The book was a periodic Autobiography that I thought was worthwhile to share with the world. The focal point of that book was to motivate and encourage others positively that they can overcome whatever hardships and disappointments they may be experiencing by implementing a tenacious approach as I did.

The book chronicled the reasons why I left my homeland of Jamaica and migrated to America on a leap of faith. I ventured on this journey knowing that I had no family to rely on that would acclimatize me to the American culture. Explained are the obstacles I had to overcome in adapting to a new culture during my first five years in a new environment. Coming from a predominantly black society in Jamaica, I never had to deal with racism. Detailed in the book are various encounters with racial discriminations and how I handled those sensitive situations. The drama and suspense of adjusting to a new society is detailed. Also depicted is how I exercised my faith and trust in God, to combat and defeat all oppositions that confronted me.

I am hoping that the book will achieve its objective to influence others to take action instead of waiting for things to happen. In retrospect, I can truly thank God for his timely intervention that allowed me to overcome those trying times successfully.

America is now my home, and I am proud to say that I am an American citizen. The decision I made then to leave Jamaica and the initial hardship I endured here in America has made me a better person today. Now that I am in my senior years, I sometimes reflect on some of the poor choices and bad decisions I made and the impact they have on me today.

I am now focused on moving forward with a renewed mindset to improve on my future by continuing to plant positive seed on the fertile grounds of my mind and nurture it with the expectations of a bountiful harvest. In order for me to step into my miracle territory, I will have let go of my past, renew my mind and reposition myself to receive my future blessings. "Be ye transformed by renewing your mind, that ye may prove what is that good, and acceptable, and perfect will, of God".

My priority is to focus on the importance of winning the battle of my mind. To be victorious in this area, I will be able to make better choices and decisions along life's journey. Depending on future decisions I make, the consequences will either be positive or negative and will have lasting effect.

To be assured of success along the remainder of my life's journey, I will always put God first in all my undertakings and not rely on my own understanding or experience and I will achieve tremendous success in all aspects of life. If we put our trust in God He will implant positive thoughts that will enable us to make the right decisions every time that will yield prosperity.

CHOICES, DECISIONS, & CONSEQUENCES

MY ANALOGIES OF LIFE'S JOURNEY

Our past is gone never to return. Whatever happened in our past, because of choices and decisions we made then, has influenced who we are today. We should learn from our mistakes and implement corrective methods for improvement, that our future will not be a duplicate of our negative past. What God has in front of us is better than anything that we left behind. He is always with us; whether we are experiencing prosperity or hardship from the choices and decisions we made resulting in the consequences we are now experiencing. He is our refuge, fortress and guide, through the storms and turmoil of life's unpredictable journey.

THE RED SEA ANALOGY

The reason why God parted the Red Sea was to allow the Israelites to cross over on dry land and be removed from adversity in Egypt to prosperity in the Promise Land. After they crossed over on dry land to the other side, the water returned to its natural flow. This gave them no chance to return to the adverse situations they left behind. Pharaoh's army drowned in the Red Sea in pursuit of the Israelites with the intention of taking them back to slavery in Egypt. This illustrates that God will prepare a clear path for us through treacherous waters that will separate us from our enemies and adverse situations. He wants us to move forward toward our prosperity and leave our foes and depressed circumstances behind.

It might be necessary for some of us to have a wilderness experience like the Israelites had after gaining their freedom from slavery in Egypt. Because of disobedience, idolatry and being ungrateful to God, an eleven day journey took forty years to complete. The majority of the Israelites who started the journey never reached the Promise Land. This was due to a process of elimination by death to those who did not abide by God's principles.

Knowing this history, we must be obedient to His commandments, exercise our faith and trust that He will take us to our Promise Land at the appointed time. Awaiting us there will be freedom from physical and mental enslavement that will enable us to make independent decisions. How we handle this new found freedom will depend on the choices we make that will determine what the future consequences will be.

THE DESERT EXPERIENCE ANALOGY

Along life's journey, we will encounter circumstances that can be compared to a journey through a desert. After days of walking and depleting our water and food supply, we become tired, hungry and thirsty from the sweltering heat with no relief in sight. At this juncture we have a decision to make. We can choose to turn back to the path we have already traveled or continue moving forward into the unknown. We know what we left behind will not satisfy our current needs. Then why would we want to return to a situation that will not be beneficial or rewarding to us. If the choice is to continue moving forward into the unknown, The Good Lord always has provisions for those who faithfully persevere. He will provide an oasis which is a fertile place in the desert just around the corner. It will be our refuge and provide us with shelter, water and food to satisfy all of our needs.

This analogy demonstrates that for us to achieve prosperity in life, we should always move forward and do not look back or try return to our unproductive past. Forging ahead under duress, with faith in God, will result in reaching your oasis that will satisfy all of your needs. We miss out on our blessing by giving up prematurely before realizing our prosperous destiny.

SPORTS ANALOGY

As so eloquently presented by my senior Pastor Tony Mc Coy at Hope International Church in Groveland, Florida, achieving success can be compared with a game of basketball or football that has four quarters. The first three quarters will require intensive performance at a high level, to keep pace with or forge ahead of the opponent. At the beginning of the fourth quarter, if we are ahead in the score we will have to maintain our focus and efforts and not deviate from the game plan that brought us temporary success. This attitude will ensure victory at the game's end. On the other hand, if we get in a comfort zone and become complacent with this temporary lead, then our opponent will capitalize on our lack of effort and snatch victory from our grasp.

If we are behind in the score at the beginning of the fourth quarter, then we will have to adjust our game plan and summon our physical and mental fortitude to compete at a higher level. This will require us to be more determined and aggressive with a tenacious attitude to win at any cost. This attitude and conviction will enable us to overcome the deficit in the score and have the sweet success of victory.

The essence of this analogy is that the fourth quarter is where success is determined. To be successful in life, we should not deviate from a winning formula and be prepared to make the necessary adjustments to overcome all oppositions that confront us. We should never be complacent or be contented with any accomplishment during the competitive aspects of life. With such attitude we may see a complete erosion of what we acquired in the first three quarters. With a strong conviction to win, we must persevere and be persistent with a burning desire to achieve victory. There will be no opponent or obstacle that can limit our accomplishment with this winning attitude. These principles should be demonstrated through all stages of our lives, regardless of the opposition or circumstances. With physical and mental determination to succeed, our journey through life will be victorious.

BUS ANALOGY

Life is a journey that starts where we have no control of our birth and continues to an inevitable end that we know not when, why, how or where it will occur. There will be a termination to our lives by death at some point, and where we spend eternity will be a direct result of our lifestyle here on earth.

In Jamaica, the main mode of public transportation from rural areas to the city is by bus. When we enter the bus, there will be passengers already on board that we have never met before. Later along the journey we may have the opportunity to meet and interact with some of the passengers and realize that they have different destinations. There will be various stops along this journey where some passengers will get off and others will get on. This is typical in life, where we will meet people for a brief period and they will exit our lives while new ones enter.

We may know some of the new passengers that get on and try to get their attention, but they will ignore us. Some passengers will be friendly, and we will be able to engage in sociable conversation making this journey fun and enjoyable. They will make a positive impression with us, and if they get off before we reach our destination, we will be very disappointed and miss their company. There are others on board who will be boisterous, vulgar and confrontational, and we must exercise patience and tolerance to make this bus ride pleasant. We must try to understand all people, which will enable us to determine who to associate with and who to avoid.

All passengers will have different destinations, but they cannot predict what might interrupt this travel resulting in delays beyond their control. The bus may be involved in an accident that will create delay, confusion, stress, injury and even death. If someone that we had established a good relationship with got injured or died, that would be devastating to us. In life we will lose love ones and we must learn how to overcome those losses.

These are all similar experiences that will confront us along life's journey, and we must be prepared to adjust to negative people and tragic circumstances by letting go and moving forward. How we interact and engage with all people helps to determine the quality of life we will experience.

BICYCLE ANALOGY

At the early stages of life's journey, we will be tested for our faith, patience and our ability to perform by being obedient to instructions. Learning to ride a bicycle can be a traumatic experience for a young child. It requires trust and a cooperative effort by the child with whoever the instructor is to achieve the balance and coordinated skill, to perform effectively this mode of transportation on two wheels. To prevail successfully during the early stages of learning, the child will have to overcome fear and doubt to conquer what at first seems like an impossible feat. With consistent practice, patience and a dedication to succeed, victory will be realized.

The child will eventually ride off triumphantly without any assistance. This will be very gratifying accomplishment at a young age to recognize that with conviction and sacrifice success can be achieved. This experience will sow a seed of victory over an obstacle that should manifest itself positively later in life.

A bicycle is designed to transport an individual who is well balanced and coordinated in a forward direction only. Consistent effort is required to ride successfully to the desired destination in a timely manner. To stop pedaling will slow the progress and the bicycle will eventually come to a halt. This is an indication that success is achieved through continued and consistent effort that will enable constant forward motion. With trust in God, He will empower us to triumph over all adversities, and we will ride off into prosperity through His guidance and assistance.

This analogy demonstrates that to progress effectively along life's journey, we must achieve the right balance, acquire the required skills from the right people and be persistent. These combinations will enable us to pedal up inclines, down slopes, negotiate all curves in any type of weather enabling us to reach our miracle territory.

Along life's journey we should have visions, hope and ambitious aspiration for great accomplishments. There will be challenges, disappointment and hardship that will test our resolve. In our society, prosperity and success are usually gauged by a person's material and financial accomplishment. We have a tendency to be jealous and envious of the lifestyle that these fortunate and successful people can afford to live. We never factor what sacrifices and hard work they endured to achieve this status in life. For us to attain that lifestyle, we must be willing to make the sacrifice with a conviction to succeed at any cost.

Our hindrance from being prosperous is usually a result of being associated with non-progressive people. Aspiring for success will require us to let go of things and people that we know, and are comfortable with, but they retard our progress. Because of fear, loyalty and our insecurity, we are reluctant to let go of those unproductive associations that inhibit our prosperity. We must step out this comfort zone into a more positive environment that will propel us to success. To be a winner, we must place ourselves in a winning environment, where other winners reside. We must try to make the best of our journey, interact positively with our fellow man, give generously and come to their assistance in their time of need. With this attitude, God will bless someone in our life that will come to our aid in our time of need.

CHOICES, DECISIONS, & CONSEQUENCES

THE BEGINNING OF LIFE'S JOURNEY

In the beginning, God created heaven and earth and said let us make man in our own image, after our own likeness. He then created Adam and Eve, placed them in an ultimate living environment, where they had choices in fruits, vegetables, fishes, various meat sources and had complete dominion over all living things and creatures. This couple is our lineage, and they were blessed and instructed by God to be fruitful and multiply.

They are the reason why we are here today. Because of their disobedience to God, they yielded to the temptation of the devil and committed the first sin of eating the forbidden fruit. By committing that first, sin we, being their descendents, inherited being born in a sinful world. "Indeed, I was guilty when I was born, I was sinful when my mother conceived me", but God sent his only begotten Son on earth to suffer and die for the redemption of our sins that we may have the gift of eternal life.

Before we were born, our path of destiny was ordained by God. He knew us before we were formed in our mother's womb, and we are here to fulfill His purpose of great expectation. To realize this fulfillment, we must maintain a lifestyle that is pleasing to Him. At our birth, we have no choice of our parentage, where and when we were born. Regardless of our home environment, whether wealthy, impoverish or dysfunctional, our birth was not by coincidence but through the love of God.

In our adult life, He gives us the freedom to make our own decision and we must choose if we want to walk in the path he has prepared for us or prefer to yield to the lust and desire of the flesh and indulge in worldly pleasures. If we choose to be faithful to him and walk in the path of righteousness for his name's sake, then our travel through life's journey will have God's guidance to achieve peace and prosperity. If the choice is to conform to worldly pleasure, then we will not have God's covering along life's journey and that could result in negative consequences.

Life's journey is a road of twist and turns, hills and valleys, stops and starts, and we will need God's guidance to help us to navigate these variations in the terrain to be successful. We do not know the appointed time when our life's journeys will inevitably come to an end. Our lifestyle on earth will determine where we will spend eternity.

TRAVELING THE JOURNEY

Life is a journey that starts from inception in the womb and will be terminated at our death. From a child through our senior years, we will make numerous decisions along this journey that will have consequences and will impact family, friends and other people that will cross our paths. We have a tendency to blame others for the bad choices we made when they result in negative consequences later on in life. Our destiny is generally determined by the choice and decisions we make. "I have set before you life and death, blessing and curse: choose life that thou and thy seed may live".

God tells us that life's journey was not going to be easy and that there will be many obstacles and problems along the way. These situations are very temporary and are usually a test of our faith. God could be preparing us for our break through into our prosperity. These obstacles can be viewed as deterrence or accepted as a challenge that we can overcome. "We are more than conquerors through Him that loves us".

All human possess certain definitive internal traits that are executed consistently throughout our lives. We can choose to exhibit them in a positive manner that will be beneficial in elevating us to a higher standard of life. With the assurance and a mindset of great reward, successful people display these positive qualities habitually. We are all ordained by God to be prosperous and successful. Because of insecurities, tradition and lack of faith in God we concede to a life of mediocrity and failure.

CHOICES, DECISIONS, & CONSEQUENCES

These are some of the traits that if demonstrated with confidence, knowing that The Good Lord will never leave or forsake us, we will be propelled to a higher elevation. If these qualities are properly implemented with restraint, respect and love for others we will reap bountiful harvest.

<u>CHARACTER</u> : The true character of an individual becomes evident in the manner how he handles the many obstacles he will encounter. The manner in which he approaches these obstacles will usually determine the outcome. We should not try to delegate them to others, ignore them or circumvent them but make the decision to resolve them by whatever means necessary at all times. We must be courageous, determined, persistent, and aggressive in our approach, and we will conquer the greatest obstacles that confront us. If we are passive, submissive and give up easily, we are doomed to fail. To achieve success we must trust God that He will not give us more than we can bear and recognize that He gave us dominion over all things and circumstances. We should take action to do what we can, and God will act on the things that we can't.

To achieve maximum success we must put forth our best effort and utilize our talents because "Faith without work is dead". We should be determined to complete any assignment we started, whether as an individual or in a cooperative effort.

We must be aware of who we associate with when pursuing our goal. There are those with a crab in the barrel mentality, who through envy will try to pull down progressive people to their level of mediocrity. It is imperative that we disassociate ourselves from these negative, jealous individuals and reposition ourselves to a more positive and favorable environment where people are striving for success.

ATTITUDE: Our attitude can determine our lifestyle. We should make the choice to have a positive attitude daily because circumstances are always changing. If we consistently have a confident mindset by thinking, walking and talking boldly, then we will realize fulfillment beyond our dreams.

Many decisions are made by the first impression of another person. We should always be conscious of our outward appearance which we have control over. At all times we should look our best, maintain an upright and positive posture, and always make eye contact when speaking to others. In our greeting we should always give a firm handshake with a pleasant facial expression. This approach will project confidence and a healthy self esteem with whomever we meet. We are a masterpiece created by God who was born to win, but we allow negative circumstances from the poor choices we made to overwhelm us and we succumb and accept mediocrity.

Too many times along life's journey, we elect to play it safe. This is usually due to the fear of failing. Life's journey can be equated to an elevator design for a building with twenty floors. We can make a choice to get off at the first floor or the fifth floor or continue to its ultimate height. With a positive mindset, confidence and trusting in God, we will ride this elevator to the pinnacle where an abundance of wealth, joy and prosperity awaits us. Through fear, insecurity or minor obstacles we may elect to get off the elevator before it attains its maximum height.

Fear is the biggest reason that retards our progress. We should not allow fear to inhibit our advancement towards our goal. "Yea, though I walk through the valley of the shadow of death I will fear no evil: for thou art with me thy rod and thy staff they comfort me". If we focus on this Bible passage and reinforce it daily in our thoughts, then our achievements are limitless. We must remember that God took David from the pastures to the palace. He is no respecter of person; what He did for David then, He will do for us now. By extending our faith in God, we will let Him make positive changes that will solve any problems that hinder our progress.

To be elevated from mediocrity to prosperity, we must be persistent and consistent with a sense of purpose to excel to the highest level at any cost. We should be happy for successful people and remain optimistic within ourselves, with the belief that we will reap our harvest in God's appointed time.

<u>CONFIDENCE:</u> There are constant changes in technology in all industry that contributes to our improved standard of living. As humans we naturally resist change in our personal lives because we become comfortable in our environment, our circle of friends, family lifestyle, our impression of people and things. To realize personal growth we must step out of this comfort zone with confidence, independent thinking and faith in God. We should make our own personal decisions and not rely totally on the recommendations or advice of our parents, family, or friends to direct our path along life's journey. With confidence and an independent positive thinking, speaking boldly and a strong desire with the belief that we will attain the loftiest goal we can envision, then it will be achieved. "The difference between a successful person and others is not a lack of strength, not a lack of knowledge, but rather a lack of will" (Vince Lombardi).

If our aspirations are to be wealthy then we must consistently think of being financially successful, supported by a plan and hard work in our pursuit to achieve this goal. As Henry Ford once said, "Whether you think you can or you can't do something, either way you are right". We can design and shape a future of prosperity by our thoughts and speech. "Life and death are in the power of the tongue".

We constantly have a personal internal conversation that eventually will become evident by our action. It is imperative that those internal dialogues be very positive in nature with the aspiration to achieve greatness. We then should design a plan to convert these positive thoughts into action.

We will be in company of family and friends that are pessimistic and uninspiring and because of this association we are inclined to adopt their way of life. We should exercise mental strength without malice and sever ties from individuals who are not motivated to be elevated to a higher level. If we are from an impoverished neighborhood, we don't have to be a product of that environment. We will suppress our potential for greatness if we allow negative surroundings to dictate our destiny.

To avoid being influenced by this lifestyle we must transform our mind and attitude to be more assertive in our actions, declare prosperity in our thoughts and speech, and we will be elevated to a level beyond our expectations. We should step out on faith from the limited boundaries that confine our mind and body which will restrict our progress.

GENEROSITY: Man has a tendency to focus on satisfying his own desires and dreams, and many times ignoring the plight of those less fortunate than ourselves. To achieve financial blessings we should choose a lifestyle of generosity, with a sowing and reaping mentality, and incorporate the notion of giving cheerfully of our time, effort and money to those in need. Because of selfishness and greed, we hoard and preserve our financial and property gains for ourselves. We fail to realize that all things we acquire belong to God, and our responsibility is to be good stewards of his money and possessions. This involves being accountable of his blessing to us that will enable us to be a blessing to others by giving. "For God so loved the world that he gave his only begotten son that whosoever believeth in Him should not perish but have everlasting life". This is the greatest gift mankind will ever receive, that brought pain and suffering on the cross to our Lord and Savior Jesus Christ for the redemption of our sins.

One gift that we must consistently give regardless of our financial circumstances is tithing ten percent of our income at our place of worship. This will be an investment on earth towards our heavenly kingdom. "For where your treasure is, there your heart will be also". If we obey this principle of tithing, God will open the windows of heaven and pour out a blessing that there shall not be room enough to receive it. By being disobedient to this principle is considered robbing God, and He can impose a curse where our financial accomplishment will be temporary.

The question has always been raised about the justification for tithing and offering in churches. The perception is that this money is given to enhance the lifestyle of the Pastors and their staffs. If they misappropriate our tithing for their personal use, they will have to answer to God. Purchases at grocery stores and retail businesses are never questioned because we receive the items for the cash outlay immediately. By being obedient to the principles of tithing, man will enjoy a greater reward from God in his time of need.

We should make a choice to always give lovingly and freely from the heart to the needy and poor without reservation or attitude. In order receive consistent reward as a go getter we should demonstrate a go giver attitude. God loves a cheerful giver, and the compensation from giving will be a blessing that will enable us to realize increase on what we already have. Giving is not only monetary, but volunteering our time to serving others will be equally appreciated. There are numerous organizations and churches that have programs geared to helping the underprivileged, the handicapped and the homeless where our services will be beneficial to those in need. Dedicating our time to these worthy causes, without the expectation of monetary reward, will be a blessing to those we serve and in turn we will be blessed. Jesus Christ came to earth to serve and not being served. We should try to replicate all the actions Jesus did that were of great benefit to mankind.

DISTRACTIONS: There will be many distractions along life's journey, as a result of poor choices in our finances and family issues. Financial difficulties can create tremendous stress, disrupt family life and is one of the major causes for divorce. With available financial resources at our disposal, we will spend spontaneously through enticing promotion to satisfy a want and not a need. These uncalculated acts will result in serious consequences of indebtedness later. Sometimes we will justify those bad choices by saying if we only knew then what we know now, we wouldn't be confronted with these financial woes. We must make a choice to move forward and learn how to improve on those past bad decisions. Now that the damages have been done, we should implement necessary changes to avoid repeating those poor choices.

To overcome indebtedness from our irresponsible spending, there has to be a change in our lifestyle. Some of the necessary steps to be taken are to be more aware of unnecessary spending and to use cash instead of credit card. It may be necessary to get a second job, try to be satisfied with what you currently have, and get financial counseling.

Lazy and weak-minded individuals have no patience and little faith in God that he will supply their needs if they put forth the effort to get a job. They are not willing to sacrifice their time and effort productively. They will try to resolve these financial issues on their own. They will resort to a life of crime, seeking a quick solution to their problems and totally ignoring the consequences the law will impose on them for their bad decisions.

There will be family misfortunes and circumstances such as terminal illness, disabilities, death and problems with children that can result in disunity within a family. An unfortunate situation where a family member is incarcerated for making bad choices will be stressful for the family. With strong mental and psychological attitude and unified support within the family the effect will be minimized. A God fearing family will exercise faith and patience and make decisions as a unit to overcome these unfortunate issues that will yield positive results.

A POSITIVE MINDSET: For life's journey to be successful, we must make the decision to let go of our negative past. Our future is predicated through our thoughts, attitude and speech. You cannot expect victory if you continue to speak defeat. We should always try to send out words of optimism, with the expectation of positive results. Try to look on the sunny side of everything and work to make optimism a reality. If we are experiencing difficult circumstances, do not talk about how we are currently, but what we expect to become. We should consistently make positive declarations and compliment ourselves after a task has been successfully completed. Try to forget mistakes of the past, learn their lessons and move forward to greater accomplishments in the future.

It is difficult to step through the doorway of our future if we continue to hang around the hallway of our past. "Look not mournfully in the past. It comes not back. Wisely improve on the present, it is thine" Henry Wadsworth Longfellow. If we adhere to this principle, then we will be motivated to focus on improving our current situation and letting go of past disappointments by the poor choices we have made.

We should always make a conscious decision that in order to progress through life's journey successfully; we must always look forward through the windshield of life and not backward in the rearview mirror of errors and bad decisions. If we keep looking back at the bad choices we have made, will lose sight of the prosperity God has in store for us in the future.

Our future will not be determined by luck or chances but by the choices and decisions that we make as we travel life journey. We will remain where we are if we continue to focus on our unfulfilled expectations. The hurt and pain that we endure because of poor choices should not discourage us from walking boldly in the miracle territory God has reserved for us where we will have a fulfilled, enriched and enjoyable life.

Releasing our negative past requires that we renew our mindset to focus on the positive aspect of our lives. Yesterday is gone, tomorrow is not promised to us and today is now. We should aspire to make our today an improvement on yesterday by making the right choices and decisions that will also enhance the many tomorrows to come. We should rejoice and be glad daily, formulate Godly principles with a positive mindset, with great hope and expectation for a prosperous future.

INSTANT GRATIFICATION: We are in a society where there is a desire to have positive results for our efforts immediately. We are not prepared to endure through difficult circumstances which will require persevering for a period of time to acquire our desired goal. There is great demand for a fast paced result in most aspect of today's society. In this age where social networking is done via computer, iPod, etc. dominates the method of communication indicates of the evolution of this society. This method of corresponding is very fast and effective but very impersonal and antisocial. This is a good example of the demand for quick response in our daily routine.

It is very important that we do not lose sight of the fact that patience is a virtue and should be exercised along life's journey. In our haste, we forsake the written word in the Bible "Wait on the Lord: be of good courage and he shall strengthen thine heart." Because of the urgency we impose on ourselves to achieve our set goal hastily, we make poor choices by trying to satisfy the desired objective immediately. When we realized that it is not feasible to be accomplished within that time frame, we tend to resort to improvise creative means to attain those goals as planned. These decisions are usually devised spontaneously and are not well thought out and may result in negative consequences.

Decisions should be well thought out and not based on emotions. Emotional decisions sometimes cause regrets and disappointments when we are unable to successfully accomplish those goals in a set window of time. Patience has its reward, and it should be explored diligently before making a hasty decision.

If we reflect on the Bible on what Job endured and how he exercised patience, faith and trust in God, he eventually reclaimed seven times more of what he lost. His attitude exemplified that "we can do all things through Christ Jesus who strengthens us". We should not be influenced by this hasty environment to accomplish our desired objectives at a pace that is uncomfortable for us. It is best to devise a workable plan, with a practical time frame, unleash our fullest potential, and we will achieve great success.

<u>LOVE:</u> There are various types of love relationships that are displayed to a variety of people in a different manner. Love of family, friends and affectionate love of the opposite sex are exhibit differently. Genuine love for the opposite sex should be profound, tender and passionate and should not be motivated primarily for sexual interaction. This love should be displayed through action and not by creative dialogue with the intention of achieving other ulterior objective. True love manifests itself through commitment and a genuine conviction to bring joy and happiness to another person without expecting a reward for the action.

The pursuit of love will require patience. Sometime we will encounter rejection and disappointments, but we should endure and be persistent because the right person is worth the wait. Many times we will miss out on a good relationship because we concede to what we perceive as not being at the right place at the right time. This could be a test of our sincerity and loyalty, and we lost out on a good person.

Lust should not be confused with love. Lust is an intense passionate yearning, sexual craving, or desire for another person without an emotional attachment. Lust is generally the initial attractions that sometimes develop into love. Men generally formulate their criteria for the love of a woman by their sexual appeal. The physical appearance remains the dominant reason for a man to approach a woman. An attractive face, voluptuous figure, breast projection and weight to height ratio are generally scrutinized before an approach is made. These criteria vary in men but serve as a confirmation that in general there is lust before love. The final determination will be based on the woman's judgment if there is real genuine affection that will enthuse enough to get involved.

In the Christian faith the three most recognized types of love are:

(1) Eros love is base on an arousing and satisfying sexual desire of another person of the opposite sex. This type of love is based on personal self gratification for sexual satisfaction. It is usually stimulated by lust of the physical traits of another person. This in general is the initial stage of a romantic relationship.

(2) Philos love is a relationship between two individuals based on friendship, void of any sexual or intimate encounter. There are generally common interests that facilitate this relationship. This could develop between family members, co-workers, sport activities, church members or neighbors. Sometimes this friendship between a man and a woman blossoms into an intimate relationship. After a foundation has been laid for a good friendship and a comfort zone has been established, then there is a good prospect for true love to emerge.

(3) Agape love is an unconditional love given to another person without expecting any benefits as a reward. The greatest kind of agape love is the divine and spiritual love God gave us by sending his only son Jesus Christ to die on the cross for the remission of our sins. There is no greater love than this, which has saved us from spending eternity in hell.

As we travel this journey of life we must make the choice to love our neighbor as we love ourselves. We sometimes have a misconceived notion that our neighbors are only the people living next door. That is the wrong perception because our neighbors should have no boundaries or nationalities. "There is neither Jews nor Greek, slave nor free, male nor female for you are one in Christ Jesus". We should be accommodating, receptive and helpful to all people that cross our path. As illustrated in the Parable of the Good Samaritan, who came to the aid of a complete stranger that was beaten and seriously injured? He showed compassion by comforting him and dressing his wounds. He then took him to an inn and paid for his care of his well being. Jesus referred to the Samaritan as a good neighbor and instructs us to do likewise.

There is a comfort level to display love and harmony only to people who look and speak like us. This attitude would exclude a large number of people and limit our exposure to the many different cultures and nationalities. We should make the decision to step out of the box of our own comfort zone and reach out and embrace all people. "So we being many, are one body in Christ, and everyone members one to another". By enlarging our territory, we will open opportunities we would never be aware of if we continue to limit our relationship with only people within our culture or nationality.

VISION: Life's journey is like venturing into unknown territory that will require a road map. Without this map, we will either get lost or have to ask for direction. The best road map for a prosperous and pleasant journey is called a vision. This will require that we have a positive mental attitude with a planned goal or dream that has a destination to great success. This vision should be well formulated, with the commitment and an aggressive attitude to execute it within a specified realistic target date.

A vision should not be viewed a one long race but a series of many short races to be accomplished in an orderly manner culminating in the ultimate objective. When devised in this manner there will be the opportunity to modify it that will enhance the results.

We should not allow any distraction or circumstances to divert us from this visionary path. We must have a vision of increase and victory that will gradually and methodically foster an enriched, joyful and prosperous life for ourselves, family and our future generation. "Where there is no vision people will perish". Always picture yourself as being successful and keep your eye on the prize that you aspire to attain and how rewarding it will be when it is achieved.

We should try not to be associated with individuals that have no vision. If there is nothing working towards, then there is no great expectation for their future. For anyone to improve their status of life, it will require work with a plan and an objective to get to the next level. Misery loves company, and we should avoid being associated in the company of people without a vision because they will retard our progress from fulfilling our prosperous destiny. We should make the effort to be in the company of winners at all times, where the ultimate goal is to hoist the trophy of victory after perseverance and tenacity has defeated all obstructions.

We should not let our current circumstances overwhelm us and keep us in a depressed state of mind that will prevent us from acquiring great wealth. Continue to strive forward with an optimistic attitude that greener pastures are ahead. For vision to be attainable we must have a workable incremental goal in writing and read it regularly to maintain our focus on the reward at the end of the rainbow. "Write the vision and make it plain upon the table that he may run that readth it". This vision should have a definable goal that is flexible, allowing us to refine it as we progress along the way.

The essence of a goal is that it identifies where we were before, where we are now, where we are going in the future and how we are going to get there. To achieve our goal, significant change and adjustment must be made in our priority, attitude and dedication. We must be willing to make the sacrifice for steady and consistent progress daily that will enable us to accomplish our goal. We should also receive Godly guidance from a spiritual leader to council us in formulating this goal. A knowledgeable accountability partner to monitor our progress is essential, to monitor our progress periodically.

If we apply all the principles outlined in this chapter, our journey through life will be fulfilled in all areas and we will have a harmonious relationship with our fellow humans. This should serve as a template that if implemented with confidence and faith will give us life filled with love, joy and happiness as God expects us to have.

TO LEAD OR TO FOLLOW

To be a leader, one must have the ability to guide, direct, delegate and influence their followers to a positive targeted objective. The essential qualities of an effective leader are to be of high integrity, confidence, influential, communicative, honest and trustworthy. They should have the ability to articulate the theme of the venture the organization is pursuing in a manner their followers can easily comprehend. Whenever the purpose for leading is not well presented and understood by its followers, then there is a perception of the misuse of authority that could create a problem. Whether it is in the military, a corporation, the church, our home or in politics, strong leadership qualities are required to be displayed effectively to achieve the ultimate goal of a united cooperative and improved quality of life.

Good leaders will train capable people within the organization or the group to take up the mantle should they become incapacitated or die. A preparation for a smooth transition is necessary to maintain the cohesiveness and the objectives of the desired goal.

Some of us were born with the gift of leadership; others acquire that position through promotion, some are elected, while others are appointed. Regardless of how this position is attained, for others to follow, the path of the desired destination should be clearly defined. Some of the reason why people are persuaded to be led is to serve their country, to worship and praise God, improve their education, to earn an income and to socialize.

There should be a good comfort level for interaction between the leader and those who follow. Leaders should not abuse their position of authority to dominate or demoralize those who follow. This might create an environment of fear, intimidation and doubt with regards to the achieving their objectives without any disputes. The responsibility of a good leader is to integrate, create harmony and unity that will establish long term cohesiveness. Some leaders choose to exhort their position through arrogance and being overly assertive to control their followers. Others use the gentle persuasion approach that may include a meeting to discuss different viewpoints before making a final decision.

Followers sometimes will view their leader as a role model and are expecting high morals, with class and integrity that they can adopt. These qualities will enable them to aspire to a leadership role in their future. It is important for leaders to live a good exemplary lifestyle with their family, church and in their leadership role. These traits will give the leader credibility that will enable him to sustain his position with the support of his followers for the designated tenure and the possibility of re-election for another term.

There are individuals who choose to lead for ulterior motives, with the intention of enhancing their personal ambitions. They may see the prospect of exploiting a group or organization for financial gains, achieve prominence to satisfy an ego and indulge in sexual immoralities from their followers When these motives become evident, it could result in negative repercussions, such as disunity, rebellious reaction, removal of the leader or dissolving the group.

In Atlanta Georgia, male church members accuse their pastor of homosexual abuse. This case received national publicity and shockwave rolled through the church when apparent evidence was revealed against this once highly respected spiritual leader. His spirituality or his leadership ability was never in question. His choice of association and the relationships he developed impacted his credibility negatively. This association illustrate that being a leader we should walk the high road and not be involved with anything or anyone that could tarnish our reputation.

Some people will follow a passionate and charismatic leader down the wrong path because of ignorance, greed, high expectations, or for the sole purpose of belonging and socializing. There can be serious consequences for these ignorant or selfish choices, such as financial loss, addiction to the wrong things, depression and even suicide. Before submitting oneself to be led, it should be clearly understood that the objectives are realistic, attainable and is compatible with their dreams and aspirations. Some research should be done on the background of the leader to be assured that he is sincere, genuine and have the qualifications and expertise to lead them to this visionary goal that is being pursued. The eventual objective should be compatible and a desirable goal that they all seek. When this goal is achieved, it should enhance the lives of all those who choose to follow.

CHOICES, DECISIONS, & CONSEQUENCES

CHOICES, DECISIONS, & CONSEQUENCES

CHOICES, DECISIONS, & CONSEQUENCES

THE TEENAGE YEARS

Teenage years are considered to be a rebellious period, when children are forging for independence and seeking their own identity. Parental teaching will generally dictate how the children will respond to society. A teenager who grows up in a home that emphasizes Godly principles and strict discipline fosters positive behavior and attitude in the child. Parents should make the effort to be involved in the children's decision making process. Priority should be placed on a good education that will be beneficial in their future.

Teenagers will be required to make their own choices and decisions that will determine their own future. Their selection of friends is vital at this age because they are very vulnerable to peer pressure. They will have to decide whether to associate with friends that engage in positive or negative activities. If the choice is to align themselves with friends that focus on their studies, that will enable them to graduate from high school and possiblyget a college education. If they are not academically astute, the there are other alternatives, such as learning a trade or joining any branch of the military.

It would enable them to enhance their chance of enjoying a good standard of living, being disciplined, productive and a responsible person in our society. Other benefits include the ability to command better than average paying jobs and the prospect of being promoted to a top position within their chosen profession.

Peer pressure can influence many teenagers to associate with the wrong crowd and get involved with drugs, gangs, prostitution and dropping out of school. To choose to be associated with individuals who indulge in any of these inappropriate activities would lead to an average, unpredictable and carefree lifestyle. Whatever decisions are made by the parents and the child during the teenage years will impact their future of the child.

It is the parents' responsibility to prepare their teenage children for the real world by allowing them to experience both failure and success. "Failure is simply the opportunity to begin again more intelligently" (Henry Ford). They should not do anything for their children that they cannot do for themselves. The more you do for your teenage children the things that they are capable of doing, the more they become dependent and will never realize their full potential. There should be chores assigned to teenagers with no compromise in consistency, quality of execution or accountability.

They should be made aware of the facts that all things are attainable through persistence and a positive attitude. If they are obedient to these teachings and accept responsibility for their actions, they will be rewarded positively in their adult life. This would set a precedent of good discipline and character that will enhance their chances of success.

Teenage boys' interests are divided between bonding with their male companions, trying to be intimate with their female counterparts and participating in sports. Some parents take the attitude that boys will be boys and allow their sons to have their own ways in these activities. They believe that interfering would interrupt the good times their sons are having. This would be a very irresponsible approach with a lack of parental control and discipline.

Teenage years are when an awareness of the opposite sex becomes more appealing, and there is that curiosity to explore and engage in sexual activities. As a teenager, I was very shy and reluctant to initiate any romantic approach or proposal to an admirer. I would befriend their friends with the intention of being introduced to any female prospect.

In today's society, teenage boys and girls prioritize sexual involvement as criteria for good friends. This interpretation could have serious repercussions leading to pregnancy for girls, and various sexually transmitted diseases between the sexes. The male species are created to be hunters and instinctively will say the right things to impress their potential female prey to obtain sexual favors.

The girl can choose whether to be accommodating to their sexual request or insist on a platonic relationship and refuse to indulge sexually. With a strong will and firm commitment she may decide to abstain from sex, maintain her virginity and wait until she is mentally and physically mature to be married before engaging in sex. Even at the teenage level, boys will be persistent and will resort to deceptive ploys in a believable manner and promise a girl the world in order to gain sexual pleasure.

These affairs can be very fleeting, and after he achieves his sexual objective, he will be in pursuit of a new prey. The young girl will be disappointed and hurt when she realizes that she was exploited for his sexual satisfaction. Her decision to satisfy his lust could be prompted by her desire to gain acceptance, feel loved or a result of peer pressure. These sexual encounters sometimes lead to pregnancy.

There is a high rate of teenage pregnancy, and this sometimes require that the parents to be a part of the decision making process in their daughter's best interest. There are three choices to be made:

(1) be supportive of their daughter and welcome the birth of the child. This will result in their daughter be absent from school for the birth, care and nurturing of her baby. When provision is made for home care of the baby and the young mother is physically and mentally ready then it would be in her best interest to return to school.

(2) The daughter can choose with or without the parents' knowledge to have an abortion. If this choice is made then there could be unfavorable medical consequences that could negatively affect the young mother's life permanently. To abort a pregnancy is considered taking the life of an unborn human being and is the ungodly decision to make.

(3) To give birth and later give up the child for adoption. This would relieve the young mother from caring for a child that she might not be prepared to do. This decision would benefit the desire of a couple that wanted a child that they were not able to have naturally.

In many cases teenage pregnancies has a family history. The teenager is a mother, her mother is in her 30's, her grandmother is in her 50's, her great grand mother is in her 60's and her great, great grand mother is still alive. To break this cycle of teenage pregnancy will require Godly counseling to change the mindset and a decision that will influence a change in behavior.

CHOICES, DECISIONS, & CONSEQUENCES

CHOICES, DECISIONS, & CONSEQUENCES

ADULTHOOD

At this phase of our lives, we are expected to progress in maturity, being more responsible and accountable for our conduct. If good decisions were made during the teenage years, the results should be a mature, responsible and prepared individual, ready for the workforce and parenthood. As an adult, whether a college or high school graduate, the top priority is to be consistently gainfully employed, earning a steady income and maintaining a good quality lifestyle. During their school years the decisions should have been made as to what field of endeavor they decided to pursue.

I did not have a career in mind that I intended to pursue during my high school years in Jamaica. I got my first job at age sixteen in an engineering office as a helper. My duties include filing, copying of various documents and running errands. This environment prepared me to be disciplined, cooperative and how best to interact with authorities.

As a new employee, it is important to be aware of the fact that employers' expectations are punctuality, performance at the highest level, and respect for authorities. If these criteria are consistently satisfied, then there will be the possibility for promotion and a salary increase. To ensure financial stability will require being responsible and accountable for their earnings that will impact their future. Not abiding by these principles will have dire financial consequences later in life. Job hopping in the pursuit of a higher income can be detrimental to their stability and have a negative view by prospective employers in reviewing job application. Permanency on a job will produce consistent income and provides entitlement to a good pension later in life.

Home ownership is a critical decision for residency and investment that should be a priority goal to aspire toward. The pride of home ownership for safety and privacy of the family is very rewarding. You can capitalize on tax benefits, property appreciation and status of being a home owner. To choose to continue paying rent is benefiting the landlord, and as a tenant this would not be a financially wise allocation of funds. There will be no permanence or stability in a rental property due to unsatisfactory property management or the frequency of rental increase by the landlord.

Another important decision for the individuals and family is to obtain a good life insurance. Tomorrow is promised to no one, and the possibility for untimely death or serious injury resulting in disability would be a serious financial strain on the family. A life insurance policy would alleviate most of the financial strain for the family in case of serious injury or death to the bread winner. Inheritance for the children should be a decision that is made and executed. "A good man leaves inheritance for his children's children". This would be a legacy that would be for the benefit for future generations.

If one chooses to live a worldly life of partying, drinking, irresponsible money management, having numerous relationships with opposite sex, then the financial consequences will be burdensome later. It would be prudent to devise and incorporate a sound spiritual, social and financial lifestyle that will be beneficial for the future. As we continue to mature, efforts should be made to discard all of the unproductive and irresponsible behaviors we engaged in as teenagers.

CHOICES, DECISIONS, & CONSEQUENCES

RELATIONSHIPS

The manner in which we handle the various types of relationships we will be involved in will be the most meaningful thing we will have to reminisce later in life. There will be pleasant memories that will bring smiles, and we will want to recapture those special occasions. There will be regrettable encounters that will prematurely terminate an important association with a family member or a close friend. This could be a result of lack of communication, misunderstanding, or false pride. In order for a relationship to work in harmony, it will require cooperative effort by the individuals to reach out and demonstrate respect and kindness, without expecting any reward in return.

We should not try to evaluate actions or pass judgment on others by what we perceive to be inappropriate. It is important to be good listeners and observers rather than try to dictate or demand answers from perceived infractions. If a relationship becomes strained or challenging, we should put our pride and ego aside and accept some responsibility. This attitude may appease the other person, and they will be inclined to be apologetic and share some of the responsibility.

There are various types of relationships we will be involved in as we travel life's journey. The manner in which we embrace these relationships will generally determine our lifestyle. At some point along life's journey we all will engage in spiritual, platonic, social and intimate relationships. This will include people of all ages, different nationalities and the opposite sex.

CHOICES, DECISIONS, & CONSEQUENCES

The most important of all relationship is to establish and maintain a healthy, intimate and spiritual relationship with God. If we fully embrace this spiritual relationship, we will be rewarded abundantly with a lifestyle beyond our comprehension. This spiritual walk will entail attending church regularly where the good word is preached and applying it to our daily lives. Communicate with God by praying without ceasing and reading the Bible daily will shine a light in our dark areas, bringing relief to our heavy load and making our crooked path straight.

Christians should not be shy or embarrassed to acknowledge God publicly. Dining in a restaurant or as a guest for a private occasion we should proudly but reverently say a prayer of thanksgiving to God for providing another meal for us to partake. In our daily encounter with people, we should demonstrate Godly principles by acknowledging Him in our conversation. These spiritual acts should always be practiced in our homes as a family unit to receive God's blessings and protection.

In our place of employment, it is important that we establish a good working relationship with fellow co-workers. We will be in the company of some highly educated and well trained professionals in position of authority. We should not be envious or have an inferiority complex if we are not at their level of accomplishment. We should recognize and appreciate our ability to perform and try to be the very best at our assigned position.

After graduating from drafting school in New York City, I got my first job with an established consulting company in Manhattan. I was intimidated and insecure when I observed the high quality and skill level of the other draftsmen. To improve on my proficiency I came in early, stayed late and practiced at home to accelerate the quality and efficiency of my work. I also befriended a senior draftsman who was like a mentor to me. His assistance enabled me to gradually gain confidence that further enhanced my performance and productivity.

One of the main reasons for depression is that we compare ourselves to others and have a feeling of inadequacy, if we perceive that they are progressing at a higher level than we are. We should try to adapt some of their good principles that enable them to be successful and incorporate them into our work habit. Admit to your limitations and realize that God has a purpose for each of us, and we are here to fulfill that calling.

It is very important to have a healthy social lifestyle with various friends and family to participate in different activities for the sole purpose of enjoying our lives. Our social playground should not be limited to only friends and families and those that we know but extended to others outside our sphere. These social activities should extend to different people of various cultures and economic backgrounds that will broaden our scope of life. There should not be any limitation to our friendship. "A man that hath friends must show himself friendly". Socializing is a good way of releasing stress and distracting us from our problems and circumstances. In this age of social networking where we can correspond and meet people via the internet without knowing them personally gives us another avenue for socializing. This gives us the opportunity to broaden our social territory from the comfort of our homes.

A platonic relationship is usually a strong friendship between a man and a woman void of intimate or sexual involvement. This is usually based on a common interest, respect for each other and a comfort level with each other to interact and share views and ideas. This type of relationship is popular in the work place, school and churches. Observers may misconstrue this bond as being intimately involved rather than a healthy social companionship between a male and female. Through social interacting and conversation this relationship will enable both parties to have a better understanding and respect the opposite sex.

An intimate relationship is a very powerful affectionate and emotional bond between a man and woman that sometimes lead to marriage. From our teenage years through our senior years, we will need a strong intimate partner to complete and fulfill a life of joy and happiness. This person will be our confidant and trusted partner in all aspect of our life. This is a relationship we all seek and will venture to obtain the right partner to share this beautiful experience with. Once this objective is achieved, we must make the necessary effort to sustain the intimacy of this union. It will require cooperative effort towards a common goal, strong and consistent communication and forgiving each other.

To give love and receive love in return to a person of the opposite sex is an important ingredient for a healthy self esteem, pleasure and satisfaction. This type of relationship will involve sexual activities which is one requirement for a wholesome intimate union. Some people engage sexually for pleasure, others for the purpose of having children while most with the intent to enhance a long lasting relationship. God created man and woman to live happily together as a unit, to multiply and replenish the earth.

The church is a place of worship, where its members fellowship spiritually and socially. There are various groups within the church that are composed of male only, female only or both sexes together participating in spiritual worship. Whether in the choir, being an usher or a deacon, the objectives are to establish harmony within the church. Social interaction is essential and wholesome, where church members and their families can share their views and have fun in a relaxed environment.

CHOICES, DECISIONS, & CONSEQUENCES

Members will engage in social activities that include picnics, visit theme parks and attend gospel concerts that will include family members and friends for the purpose of fun and enjoyment. Recreational activities within the church family will appeal and convert unsaved people, knowing that living a Christian life can be fun and exciting while serving and praising God.

Our choice in establishing any kind of relationship in many cases will determine our life style. We must evaluate who we associate with on the basis of compatibility, loyalty, trust and personality traits. It is important to determine who to embrace for a season and who to associate with for a lifetime. These decisions will be vital in the future because a bad choice in any relationship usually have regrettable consequences. There are usually early warning signs to a bad relationship that should not be ignored. When these signs are recognized, it is our responsibility to terminate this relationship before it is fully established that will eventually result in negative consequences.

CHOICES, DECISIONS, & CONSEQUENCES

CHOICES, DECISIONS, & CONSEQUENCES

THE FAMILY

The ideal family starts when a couple gets married for the right reasons. This is when both parties are sincere and genuine about each other and are compatible spiritually, emotionally, and physically with true love and affection. If all these qualities are established and both are comfortable with each other, then this relationship is built on a solid foundation. It is very important that both parties are willing to compromise and make sacrifices to enhance this relationship. When all these criteria are satisfied, then the time is right for an expansion of the family to include children.

The husband is the head of the household and should be the provider and protector of the family. He should honor his wife, make her feel special, loved and show her know how much she means to him. "Husband love your wives, even as Christ also love the church and gave himself for it". The wife is the nurturer and is responsible to manage the home and care for the children. She should be caring, affectionate and responsive to her husband's needs. "Wives, submit yourselves to your husbands as unto the Lord". For a marriage relationship to be successful, all these traits should be consistently demonstrated.

When there is a comfort level in their finances then a desirable place of residency is critical for the proper upbringing of their children. The parents should prioritize their responsibilities to instill good values that will enhance discipline, respect and character in their children that will materialize at adulthood. They should demonstrate their affection and love for each other in an honorable way in the presence of their children as a good example for them to follow.

CHOICES, DECISIONS, & CONSEQUENCES

There should be a sense of oneness and unity within the family in all forms of activities. Compromises and forgiveness should be exercised in order to maintain a good relationship between wife and husband. They should decide on the course of action that they believe will maximize the best result for their children. For these milestones to be attained, the parents need to remain married and maintain a good interactive relationship between themselves and their children.

There will be disagreement and disputes in every family. The manner in which they are resolved will determine the stability and future of the union. Some of the issues that contribute to separation or divorce are: one person trying to be domineering over the other, spousal abuse, adultery, finances, drugs and alcoholic abuse. All these issues can lead to verbal and sometimes physical confrontations.

It is very important that these altercations do not involve or take place in the presence of the children. The mindset of children is very vulnerable, and these behaviors can be interpreted as the proper manner of settling disputes and the children are likely to display these behaviors towards their spouse in their adult life. If for any reason there are major issues that cannot be resolved and the parents decide to divorce, that would have a devastating consequence on the children. The ideal situation would be for the children to be raised by both parents from a financial and psychological standpoint.

In the case of divorce or separation, the children usually remain at home with the mother. Because of a major reduction in earning from only one salary, there would be limitation on social and recreational activities for the children. It would require closer scrutiny on the budget that would impact groceries, school supplies, and choices in college. In many cases because of the tight budget, the mother is forced to do a second job. In so doing this will affect behavioral problems with children because there will be less parental oversight and more freedom for children to do their own thing. It is widely believed that when a home is not headed by a father, there is a high rate of school dropout, a higher percentage in drug use, children are more likely to be involved in the juvenile system and have an association with negative activities.

If the dissolving of the marriage is in a civil manner and the father chooses to be responsible, then he would contribute financially to the well being of his family. Arrangement would be made where the father would have periodic custody of the children. On the other hand, if it was a unpleasant divorce and the mother made a choice to pursue financial support through the court this process could possibly have a mental and psychological effect on the children.

The best solution for the family is that the parents try to resolve their differences through counseling. This will enhance the possibility of forgiveness and compromises being displayed, enabling reconciliation of the marriage. This solution would be a good example for the children of how to resolve differences in a civil and respectful manner.

CHOICES, DECISIONS, & CONSEQUENCES

CHOICES, DECISIONS, & CONSEQUENCES

PARENTING FOR THE JOURNEY

Parents are the origin and foundation of any family. To be classified as parents would be the result of a couple of the opposite sex established an intimate relationship and through sexual involvement produce a child. Parents come in various age groups and from mixed nationalities.

In many cases the initial stage of a relationships between a man and a woman are the result of introduction through mutual friends, co-workers, family members or schoolmates. Through this meeting the stage is set for a period of dating where they will get to know each other better by engaging in various social activities. When a comfort level is established and the protective defenses are lowered, it is an indicator that a good and trusting relationship has emerged. With trust, compatibility and sincerity over time this sometimes leads to marriage. In many cases, couples may choose to live together without getting married.

Eventually over time pregnancy may occur. The expectant mother should make conscious decisions regarding proper nutrition, periodic medical checkup, a healthy diet and abstaining from alcohol and drugs. Taking these precautions will enable a healthy birth of the child. Irresponsible behavior during pregnancy can be detrimental to the unborn child in the form of physical, emotional and mental deficiencies.

After the child's birth, parents will make choices and decisions that will affect that child positively or negatively throughout the rest of its life. The mother's prime responsibility is to care, nurture and discipline the child from infancy through adolescence. The father is considered the priest of his home and his main functions are to protect and provide for the family.

As a child, I was very fortunate that my parents had a loving and caring relationship that transcended to their children. My father exemplified the true priest of our home by being a dependable provider and exhibited good leadership qualities. My mother never had to work outside the home, and she nurtured and displayed maternal affection to her four children.

Parents are responsible to make the right food choices that will produce the best nourishment as growth increase. Proper medical care is vital to ensure good health for the child. Correct decisions in all these areas will be effective for the child well being for the rest of its life. Inattentiveness to these situations will have consequences that range from poor health, inadequate development and mental retardation.

The first chance a child gets at social interaction with their peer group other than family members will either be at day care or kindergarten. This will also be their introduction to a learning facility where they will be taught by a complete stranger. Discipline, attentiveness, behavior, and obedience will be the focal point of their initial education. At first the child may have a feeling of abandonment by their parent for leaving them in a strange environment that will be demonstrated by crying. As the child gets more acclimatize to this new environment, their comfort level will improve. Children will be impacted socially and academically from these institutions at a very early age. This experience will prepare them for things to come.

It is important to instill Godly principles in a child at an early age that should yield positive results in their adult life. Bad decisions during these early years transcend generations. Behavior and attitudes by parents will be adapted and accepted by the child as the proper manner of conducting themselves and will be demonstrated later in life. Children tend to be copy cats of their parent's lifestyle and this become very evident in teenage years. "Train up a child in the way he should go: and when he is old he should not depart from it".

Parents have a choice of walking in the ways of the Lord or living a life pursuing pleasure and material gains. If the choice is a Christian way of living, that will require attending church regularly, praying and reading the Bible as a family. These behaviors will instill good Christian values in the children. The usual results will be obedience to their parents, respect to adults, disciplined behavior and not being easily influenced into improper indulgence by their peers. If the parents decide to lead a worldly life that include alcohol, drugs, partying, adulterous behavior and disrespect for each other then naturally the child will be influenced by these negative behaviors.

Usually the child will try to duplicate these actions that will result in dire consequences that could lead to unfulfilled educational achievement, constant interaction with law enforcement and being addicted to the wrong substances. These behavioral issues, if not reformed before adulthood will impact their earning potentials and the quality of life for their future family.

CHOICES, DECISIONS, & CONSEQUENCES

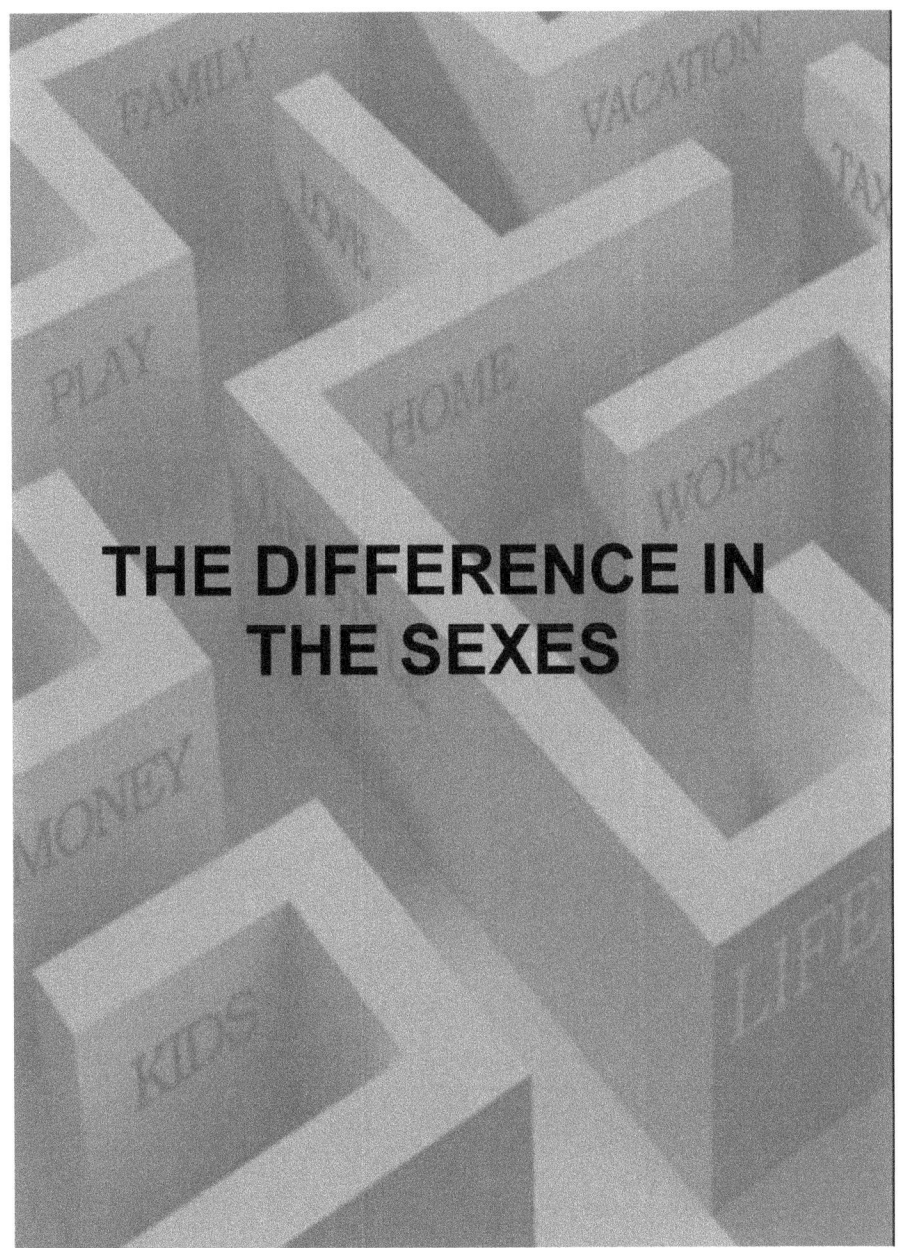

CHOICES, DECISIONS, & CONSEQUENCES

THE DIFFERENCE IN THE SEXES

There are obvious and distinct differences between male and female. Physically, men in general are more muscular, bigger and stronger than women. With these qualities men are their protector, provider and are required to do the lifting, moving and installing the various objects in and around the home. Women are considered the weaker vessel, not because of their lack of physical strength, but they are specially designed by God to be in position with a purpose to complement their male companion.

Women are the mood setters, by their ability to create the right atmosphere for most occasions. Whether it is social, formal or intimate, the guests or individual will feel welcomed, invigorated and stimulated for the occasion. In an intimate relationship women are better thinkers and planners and will stay awake at night while their spouse sleeps devising various plans of action. Most are for the betterment of the relationship, while others are of the devious nature to capitalize on a situation.

Mothers generally choose to be more protective and tolerant with their daughters at a young age. The relationship between mother and daughter is very close, and she gives guidance and counseling of how to be a physically presentable and well groomed as they advance in age. This bond will continue through adulthood where the role will reverse when the daughter becomes protective of her mother. Young girls are prepared by their mother at an early age for motherhood by the toys they play with. Their toys are comprised of dolls, household items and cooking utensils that will be her primary responsibility as a housewife.

CHOICES, DECISIONS, & CONSEQUENCES

Fathers tend to bond with their sons because it is perceived that they have more in common. They will participate in his favorite outdoor pastime that varies from playing sports, hunting and fishing. These activities prepare the boys for the outdoor lifestyle. Their toys include guns, automobile, tools and sporting items. The mother will try to teach her sons basic domestic duties, such as cooking and ironing, that will enable them as an adult to be self sufficient and independent.

As girls enter the teenage years, they are viewed by their male counterparts as sex objects. It will be the girl's decision to entertain or reject those sexual advances. The commercial world also views young attractive women as sex objects and exploits them while promoting their products. Most advertisements in the printed media or television feature women in revealing attires, regardless of the product they are promoting. They are well compensated financially for these promotions, and many will choose to make a career from this venture.

As adults, females tend to bond closely with their female family members or female friends. They will confide their most sensitive and personal matters to them without any reservation. If they are in a bad marital relationship, they will rally their female family members and friends for advice and support. These actions usually gives comfort and stress relief during these tense periods in the relationship.

Under the same circumstances, men with their big egos will choose to try to tough it out on their own. This macho attitude usually results in negative consequences. They will resort to alcoholic or drug abuse and adultery as a distraction from their situation. When these efforts do not bring the desired relief, then their mental attitude will be in a state of depression, isolation, suicidal tendencies or, in extreme cases, murder of their spouse.

Women will bond together as a group and attend various functions and activities without being accompanied by any male. They will plan trips and go on vacation as a group for the sole purpose of having good time. If they are in a dancing setting, it is not unusual to see two females dancing together and no one will question their sexuality. But if two males were to dance together, then the assumption would be that they are homosexual.

Females by nature have a tendency of being more observant, paying close attention to detail and being more verbally expressive than men. Because women are more inclined to be talkative, this may create a perception by their husbands that they are nagging housewives. In most verbal exchange at home, the wife usually wins and for a peaceful life the husband will concede and resort to watching sports on the television.

Men in general are pleasure seekers and respond visually while women make decisions through cognitive processes. Women are very conscious of their sex appeal and are aware of the fact that men are visually stimulated. Some will wear sexy, revealing attire to flirt or try to impress a potential prospect for a date. This approach will capture the imagination and attention of most men. It will be a temptation that most men will find hard to resist and will become a helpless victim.

Men are generally more aggressive in the pursuit of an intimate relationship. They will initiate a conversation to get a female prospect attention. The general theme of this first encounter will focus on impressing her with his intellect, his financial capabilities to entertain her socially and romantic dialogue to stimulate her emotionally. The main objective of this initial meeting, is to obtain a future date that will enable him to establish a platonic relationship that will hopefully develop into a romantic affair.

Women are very self conscious about their physical appearance and spend a lot of time and money on their hair, nails, fashion and a wide variety of make-up products. Because of this, the vast majority of the media advertising caters to female products. At any fashion show most of the models will be females promoting the latest seasonal fashion. The media does not promote men's fashion as much because they are not as transient as women.

The purchase of most items provides a wide contrast in the process before the final decision is made to acquire the product. The process of shopping for clothing is a good example of the contrast between the sexes. Men usually know what they want, get a fitting and are out within an hour. For a woman the same process may take her hours. First, she will window shop, then browse within the store, then try on many dresses before making a choice. Before making a final decision, she may require the approval from another female. In the purchase of real estate men tend to focus on the entertaining areas and the lot size. For a woman the kitchen, bathroom and closets will be the points of interest. The woman eventually will be the deciding force behind the purchase of the family residence.

One of the reasons why women outlive men is because of their diligence relating to medical health. She will not hesitate to visit her doctor at the first sign of any irregularity in or on her body. With this proactive approach corrective measures can be taken to treat any problem in the early stages. Men are not as in tune with their bodies as women and have a tendency to portray the tough guy image and ignore early medical warning signs until it is too late. When they finally get medical attention, the problem maybe out of control and cannot be remedied.

Men and women were created to be different and to achieve a peaceful co-existence, many compromises will have to be made to establish harmony, unity and happiness. Both sexes need each other for a complete, fulfilled and enjoyable life. This includes companionship, as a spouse, friend and helpmate that will ensure a pleasant trip through life's journey.

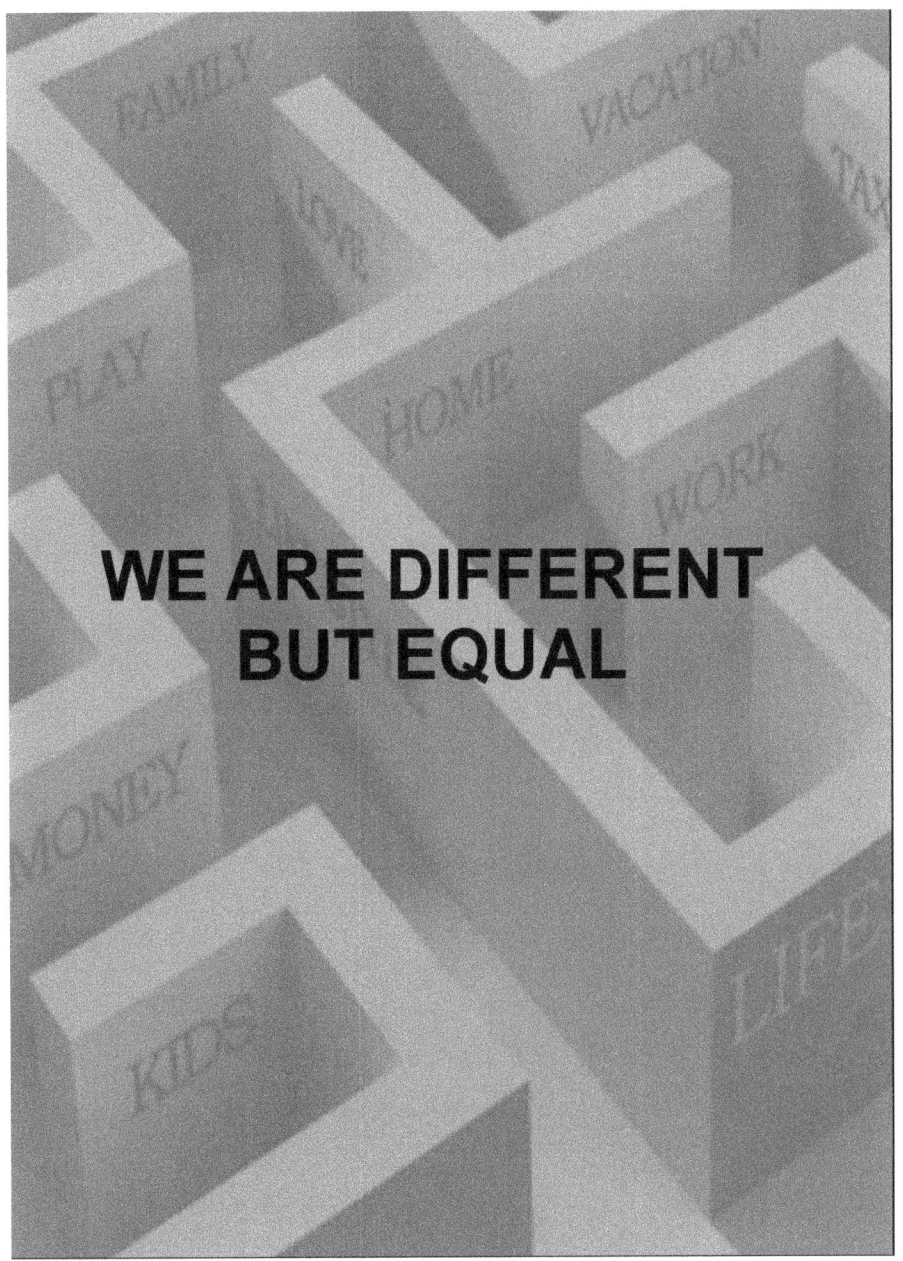

CHOICES, DECISIONS, & CONSEQUENCES

WE ARE DIFFERENT BUT EQUAL

To be different does not mean any person is superior to the other because of their difference in origin. We are all created equally by God, to love our neighbor as we love ourselves. There are some people that choose to demonstrate superiority status over their fellow man because they are convinced that they are at a higher level. These determinations sometimes are derived from their financial, racial, educational or ethnic background. They will demean and persecute those who do not look like them, speak their language or of the opposite sex. These discriminatory behaviors have created a rift, confrontation and resentment that continue to linger and may require divine intervention to resolve.

Along life's journey our paths will be crossed by many people of different race, sex, religion, culture, age and profession. It is critical for us to recognize that we are all one people to respect and interact with each other in a Godly manner. "I call upon you to draw from the depth of our being-to prove that we are a human race, to prove that our love outweighs our need to hate, that our compassion is more compelling than our need to blame" (Elizabeth Taylor). With patience and effort to understand each other regardless of our differences, this journey though life will have less confrontation and better personal relationship.

The United States has the most diverse multicultural population in the world with people from numerous countries speaking different languages and having different priorities. We must be prepared to compromise and adapt to the difference in the variation of people and situations. We should try to enlarge our territory that will broaden our scope and enhance the pleasure with a variety of people along life's journey.

RACIAL SEGREGATION: This separate and discriminatory way of life in the South has been the focal point of this country's history for a very long time. This was a deliberate effort and in some cases instituted way to keep the races separate and unequal. Because of segregation, black people were not welcomed in the better neighborhoods or the better schools and were paid less wages for performing equal tasks. They encountered humiliating and degrading circumstances that relegated them to enter through the back door of many establishments and had to ride in the rear of buses. To cope with these demeaning ways of life must have created a sense of low esteem. They were subjected to verbal and physical abuse that must have created a sense of fear and intimidation.

During the 1960's, there were united organized oppositions through peaceful marches and demonstrations against Racial Discrimination. The mood during that era was to establish equality between the races. Through determined Black leadership and with the cooperation of moderate whites, they formed the civil rights movement. This movement composed of people of different races from all over the country that took their opposition to the South where it had the greatest impact. These activities brought more awareness to the manner in which Blacks were deprived of their equal opportunity that would enable them to reach their fullest potential.

This resulted in laws being amended to facilitate the improvement of their standard of living. Because of the bold and determined action of the civil rights movement then, our society has transformed itself where today Blacks and Whites live peacefully together with love and respect for each other.

There is still some resistance by the older generation in certain section of the country that refuses to accept the benefits of an integrated society. A small pocket of whites want to revert back to the bad old days of racism. They are reluctant to acknowledge that progress has been made by all people working together to achieve a common goal of a prosperous America.

The election of our first black President is a testimony to the improvement in race relations and the acknowledgement by many whites that a black man is capable of leading our nation. With whites being in the majority, President Obama would not have been elected without their support. The civil rights era exemplifies that with a Godly approach, unity, determination and perseverance, this nation has overcome centuries of segregation and superiority oppression.

<u>SEX DISCRIMINATION:</u> Male domination has permeated all facets of our society for years and is alive and well today. Women are not only perceived as the weaker vessel physically, but as inferior in the work place and not deserving of equal pay for performing similar tasks as their male counterparts. In many establishments, women will have all the academic credentials and training that will enable them to get into management positions but are denied the deserved salary.

The world acknowledged the great potential that women possess when great nations such as Israel elected Golda Meir and Great Britain Margaret Thatcher as Prime Ministers for their respective countries. The United States appointed Madeleine Albright as their first female as Secretary of State. With these women in positions of international power, it has justified the fact that women were capable of leading and making important international decisions. These women were very influential in world affairs and during their tenure they were respected by their male counterpart from the major military and financial powers for their leadership astuteness.

CHOICES, DECISIONS, & CONSEQUENCES

There is still a psychological institutional glass ceiling, indicating that women have a limitation in position they can ascend to within the corporate structure. If this mythical glass ceiling is believed to be real, then it will be a self fulfilling prophesy that there is a limit to their ascension. Some women with strong mental and determined attitudes challenge this institutional barrier and achieve what are their rightful status and salary.

Other women will resort to deviant sexual behavior to gain favor from their superior male authority. They will flirt and seduce their male boss into engaging in sexual activities, expecting to be rewarded with preferential treatment, promotion that will increase in salary. In some cases these women will use this affair to blackmail their superior if they renege on their promise.

Women are at a disadvantage of becoming a successful entrepreneur. The government has established programs such as Small Business Association to create more opportunity for women businesses. This creates equality in the business world that has increased the earning potential of many females. If a single woman lives in a upscale neighborhood, owns an expensive luxury car and display an opulent lifestyle may give the perception that it is obtained through illicit activities and not earned through legal employment means.

Women are not treated equally for services rendered by male-dominated technicians. If there are repairs or general maintenance needed for the home of a single female, she will generally pay more than her male counterpart. The same is true for automobile repairs. There is a slow and gradual improvement in the mindset of this male dominated world to accept females as their equal in all aspects of life.

HISPANICS: In our diverse society, there has been a steady increase in the Latino population in America over the last decade. With this explosion, there is a need for all Americans and other immigrants to extend their love and welcome them as an important integral part of our society. Most are very loyal and hard working and give maximum effort at all times to perform at a high level in various industries that enhance the growth of this country's economy. Unfortunately there is a tendency of some people to have a negative stereotype attitude to all Spanish-speaking immigrants, regardless of their origin. The typical assumption is that all Spanish speaking persons are either a Puerto Rican or a Mexican. This assumption is resented by other Spanish nationals that their origin is not recognized.

The recent high profile media coverage of Mexicans entering the country illegally has impacted the Latino community. This situation has captivated the nation's attention and has caused discrimination and confrontation in some states.

There has been illegal entry into this country by Europeans, Asians, Middle East and Far East countries, but none has ever received the scrutiny and negative press coverage that the Mexicans are presently getting. Latinos make up a small percentage of mainstream media and has little influence in how they are portrayed.

Latinos are generally perceived as hard working individuals for manual type labor only. They are very visible in the various outdoor construction industries and are typecast in those positions. They will accept low paying jobs that natural born Americans do not want, and this is a big boost to the economy and the various industries. The perception is that they are not capable of being in authority with the ability to delegate to others. The truth is they occupy high ranking position, including the Supreme Court, all levels of politics, leadership roles in major corporations and various professions. All men are created equal and if given equal opportunities, they are capable of performing similar tasks successfully.

A DIFFERENT LIFESTYLE: There is a worldwide awareness and acknowledgement of the impact and influence of the homosexual population. The effort they are making to be integrated and be accepted without prejudice in all aspects of society is received with skepticism by many. They are more visible and vocal in promoting their agendas to influence more people to be sympathetic and understanding of their way of life. Homosexuals are discriminated against, because of their affinity for same sex relationship that is considered repulsive and unacceptable by many.

The three main categories for sexual involvement are heterosexual, bi-sexual and homosexual. Heterosexual relationship was ordained by God when He created the first couple Adam and Eve and placed them in the Garden of Eden. This male and female couple is our example of a perfect union for the purpose of intimate companionship and to be fruitful and multiply. This is the acknowledged, recognized and accepted relationship in most society today. To be involved in any other form of intimate relationship is considered to be violating Godly principles.

A bi-sexual relationship is when individuals are involved intimately with both female and male partners at the same time. In general this type of relationship is discrete and very low profile. Those who engage in this act could be perceived as being confused. That is because they are not committed to either a male or a female to satisfy their sexual gratification and companionship

A homosexual relationship is composed of either two men or two women as lovers. Homosexual men are referred to as gay while the women are referred to as lesbians. They are not always given equal opportunity in the workplace, sports activities or learning institutions to prove that they are capable of competing in all aspects despite their sexual preference. Some people are skeptical to publicly welcome them as equal and refrain from interacting or socializing with them. Because of this discriminatory attitude against homosexuals, they will try to conceal their behavior to avoid being ostracized.

If an individual recognizes or suspects that he/she has homosexual tendencies, he will be reluctant to disclose his feelings to family members or friends for fear of being ridiculed. If it is eventually revealed, this would be a closely guarded secret for fear of rejection and shame from their community.

In all branches of the American military, there was a policy restricting the public disclosure of homosexual on active duty. This policy is called "don't ask, don't tell". It was instituted because the defense department believed that they pose a great risk to the morale, discipline, harmony and fighting capability of their comrades. Through Congressional legislation, this law has been repealed, enabling homosexuals to serve in all branches of the military without concealing their identity.

In the private sector, homosexuals have elevated themselves to various levels of authority, enabling them to lobby their cause to influence change. In some states, there are propositions for same sex marriage that has sparked confrontation and controversy. This has resulted in major media coverage that has prompted debate and conversation from all segments of our society.

Another area that is of concern is their desire to adopt children. Since same sex unions cannot produce children, then they may resort to adoption. This notion of adoption is met with resentment by many for fear that this will influence the children to their way of life.

Despite the opposition to the homosexual way of life, we as Christians should recognize the person as a fellow human being. They should be respected, loved and welcomed as a child of God. Their choice in sexual preference should be respected but not embraced or endorsed because this is deemed improper and ungodly.

CHOICES, DECISIONS, & CONSEQUENCES

<u>RELIGION</u>: There are various religious sect within our society with different ideals regarding worshipping and who is the true God. The variety in religions generally originates from different cultures, regions or ethnicities. There are many different religions in America to choose from. The most popular are Christianity, Judaism, Atheist, Islam, Buddhism and Hinduism.

As Christians we should not be distracted or dissuaded or even challenge the views of different religions. The Christian faith expects us to focus on Jesus, the son of God, who shed his blood on the cross for the remission of our sins. We should lead an exemplary lifestyle that showcases the true virtue of Christianity by extolling Jesus as Lord and savior, loving and being generous to all mankind.

Today our society is engrossed in drugs, alcohol, violence, pornography, and homosexual behaviors. We as Christians should be more active and visible with a mission to change the attitudes and behaviors of these people to a more civil and spiritual lifestyle. To be true ambassadors for Jesus, our agenda should be concentrated on saving souls, encouraging hearts, changing communities and individuals spiritually.

Unfortunately today, it is obvious that there is less reverence for God as demonstrated by governing officials, opposed to prayer and other displays of religious symbols and activities in learning institutions. Previously, these Godly principles were considered the norm in these venues. In an attempt to be politically correct to those that oppose these Christian principles in public places, laws were changed to appease the vocal minorities. These are principles the founding fathers would not recognize today. These changes serve as a confirmation that our spiritual virtues and reverence for God is on the decline.

CHOICES, DECISIONS, & CONSEQUENCES

<u>SENIORS:</u> A good analogy for the duration of our life here on earth is from sunrise to sunset. This relates to from we were born until the time we die. As we journey through the various stages of our life, we eventually will enter the final phase which is our senior years. This is a period of gradual physical and mental decline, and we become more reliant on others for assistance. This current generation does not give honor and respect to our seniors as the previous generations did. The youth should try to learn from the vast knowledge and experience our seniors have acquired over the years. That would educate them on how to make better choices and decisions that will benefit them later on in life.

Due to advances in medical science and more awareness of the importance of proper nutrition and exercise, there is an extension to life. This has resulted in an increase in the senior population today. They are more active than their predecessors and are active participants in sports, recreation and spiritual activities.

As our society ages, there will be many seniors who will be without family assistance the financial resources to properly take care of themselves. There will be many that require mental and physical attention, and we should volunteer our time and efforts to ensure that those needs are satisfied.

Some seniors will need financial assistance for their accommodation at nursing homes or other assisted-living facilities. It is imperative that they have proper care and food that will enable a good quality lifestyle. We should make the decision to reach out and touch our seniors in whatever capacity we are capable to make them feel loved.

Now that I am a senior, my desires are to reach out and volunteer my service and money to assist my fellow comrades in need. I intend to better manage my time that will enable me to fulfill this aspiration. "I shall not pass this way but once. Therefore any good thing that I can do or any kindness that I can show, let me do it now for I shall not pass this way again" (Stephen Grellet). I believe that if we reach out and extend generosity and compassion to others, we will be rewarded in like manner.

These goodwill gestures could be an investment that will be very beneficial to us in our senior years. We should bear in mind that growing old is not an option but a natural progression in life. If we keep on living, we will eventually get old and maybe in need of assistance. If we lead a wholesome, health conscious and godly life, we will enjoy our senior years.

CHOICES, DECISIONS, & CONSEQUENCES

CHOICES, DECISIONS, & CONSEQUENCES

WHY WE GET MARRIED

There are choices and decisions to be made regarding whom we should marry, when is the right time to get marry and are we financially, emotionally and spiritually ready for marriage. If all these components are comfortably in place, then there is the prospect for longevity in this marriage. The ideal marriage is a result of a couple falling in love with Godly intentions of loving, sharing, forgiving, making compromises, and be committed to their wedding vows of "until death do us part". For a marriage to be enjoyable, exciting and long lasting, a level of trust, respect and honor should be given by both parties at all times.

Sexual activities are a very emotional, gratifying and essential aspect of this relationship. It should not just to satisfy our lustful desire or for a physical release. This should always be for a very special occasion when both parties can emotionally and physically express their love in a very intimate way and both parties will be fulfilled and satisfied after the experience. There should not be a rejection for sex as a revenge for an incident that upset either spouse. This attitude could create an unpleasant and argumentative atmosphere in the bedroom.

All marriages are not joined together with the right intentions. Some involve ploys and schemes to gain the attention and affection of their prospective partner for personal gains. In these cases there is no emotional or affectionate attraction by the pursuer, but a desire to exploit their potential spouse to satisfy their unscrupulous intentions. These marriages are usually motivated by financial greed or for status symbol recognition of their targeted partner. If this pursuit is successful then these types of relationship usually is very temporary. Then plan

"B" would be activated to acquire as much financially during the inevitable divorce settlement.

A ploy that some females use to entrap their mate into marriage is through the birth of a child. During the dating stages of a relationship, if the woman senses any reluctance by her boyfriend to get marry, she deliberately tries to get pregnant by discontinuing the use of any birth control formula and the use of anything that will enhance pregnancy. The intentions are that the prospect of fatherhood will persuade her boyfriend into marriage. She believes that the birth of child would galvanize the relationship and influence him into marrying her. If she is successful with child birth, there is no guarantee that this would ensure a permanent marriage.

In some Asian and Middle Eastern countries, many marriages are planned by the parents for their children. This is usually for the purpose of continuing a family tradition, religion, status or race. The children would have little or no choice in the matter but to honor their parents' decision. These young couples are usually teenagers and in general are obedient to their parents' desires. Sometimes the first meetings of these young couples are usually when they are introduced by the parents. The parents will hope that this meeting will be appealing to both making it easier for a smooth marriage. After the parents get their wish it will be the couple's decisions to determine if they are compatible enough for a long lasting marriage.

Foreigners who enter this country without a permanent visa, will try to pursue an American citizen through financial arrangements or try to establish an intimate relationship with the hope that it will lead to marriage. Marrying an American citizen will entitle a foreigner to legally obtain a permanent visa after being processed by immigration authorities. The intent is to acquire a green card to obtain legal residency in this country. In many cases after the desired goal of obtaining the visa is attained, the marriage will be dissolved because it was not established on a foundation of love. Since the 9/11 catastrophe by the terrorists, the immigration authorities are scrutinizing green card applications more closely for these fraudulent cases. This scrutiny will not dissuade determined immigrants who want to make America their home.

While dating my wife, who is a natural born American, question were raised about my sincerity in the relationship. There were those who thought that my intent was to exploit her to obtain my green card. She had no doubt because of the genuine love and affection I constantly displayed. We got married and lived a happy and fulfilled life.

Age disparity has always been an appealing reason for marriage. Older men trying to restore their youth or satisfy an ego will pursue women who are young enough to be their daughter with the intention of getting married. They want to prove that they still have the ability to satisfy a younger woman intimately and socially. The reverse where an older woman would try to influence or seduce a young man eligible to be her son is very infrequent.

Young women will view older men as being financially secure who can fulfill that mythical sugar daddy image. Some are seeking a father figure that they can learn from an experienced mature person how to be a better responsible individual. When the desired principles and qualities are recognized, they will try to pursue or seduce this prospect into marriage. In either case, the sincerity of this type of marriage is always questionable.

There is a big debate about same sex marriage, whether it is ethically or spiritually correct. There has been an aggressive move by homosexuals to disclose publicly their desire for same sex marriage. They continue to promote and lobby for the justification of same sex marriage. Some states have legalized this procedure which has brought strong opposition from various sectors in our society. This union is considered ungodly and would be rejected by most religious groups. Whether this type of relationship ever will be accepted by the masses is yet to be determined.

CHOICES, DECISIONS, & CONSEQUENCES

CHOICES, DECISIONS, & CONSEQUENCES

CHOICES, DECISIONS, & CONSEQUENCES

WHY SOME DON'T STAY MARRIED

There is a very high rate of divorce in our society today. The Americans for Divorce Reform estimates that probable 40% to 50% of marriages will end in divorce. For marriages to endure the inevitable trying times, will require that couples are compatible, willing to forgive and compromise to ensure permanence in marriage. If these qualities are not consistently implemented then there is the likelihood for divorce.

The reasons for the failure in many marriages vary. Some are the lack of commitment, finance, domestic abuse, unfaithfulness, and poor choice of spouse and family interventions can terminate a marriage permanently. When any of these circumstances becomes pronounced and there is no determined effort in trying to restore and preserve that high emotional and affectionate period during the early stages of the relationship, then interest begins to wane. Initially most of these marriages had good intentions of loving, respecting, compromising and willing to make the necessary sacrifices, to achieve the ultimate milestone of a long harmonious relationship. The desired goal would be to spend their senior years reminiscing of the good times they had when they were younger.

Later on along this journey of marriage, there were decisions made by either party, through selfishness, greed, adultery or reckless spending that manifest itself and the wronged party refused to forgive. Because of this unforgiving attitude, the result usually is disunity and constant arguments. These bad decisions sometimes may result in irreparable damages that affect both parties emotionally, mentally and financially. In an unhappy stressful state at home, the couple will masquerade their true feelings to the public, giving the impression that they have a happy marriage, even though they are both hurting.

There are various reasons given for remaining in this unhappy union. It's best for the children, maintaining their status within their place of worship, employment or through family pressure. Their desire to please and appease others will take priority over the ill effect of the negative relationship they are tolerating. In some cases, they need each other financially because neither can afford to be self sufficient without the other. Sometimes it is protecting certain valuables for sentimental reasons.

There will come a point when stress becomes unbearable and they will recognize there is a need for intercession by a third party. They may elect to be counseled by specialists or their spiritual leader to help bridge the gap in this dispute. In many cases these counseling sessions help to bring about reconciliation. In other cases the rift may be so divided that reconciliation is not an option by either party.

If divorce is the choice for resolving the matter, then the man stands to lose the most financially because the laws generally protect the woman. If they choose to coexist together without being divorce, then there will be a rearrangement in the behavioral pattern in the home. They will try to tolerate each other by sleeping in separate rooms, doing things and going places separately, not corresponding with opposing family. This will continue until this type of relationship becomes unbearable and the inevitable divorce takes place.

Whenever the public becomes aware that a marriage is not in harmony, the first question asked, what he did wrong. Never what did she do wrong. Society is programmed to believe that the man is always presumed guilty until proven innocent for the break up of most marriages. In many cases, when the truth is known, the reason for the disunity is because of bad choices and poor decisions by the woman that result in the dire consequences the couple are experiencing.

Women are not innocent bystanders when it comes to committing adultery. The same reasons that inspire a man to be unfaithful, such as lust, status, money, and better physical appearance of the other woman, are the same reasons that will trigger a woman to be unfaithful. If a man is having a business luncheon with another woman that is witnessed by someone who knows his wife, then the news flash will be that he was on a lunch date with another woman. If the situation is reversed, the woman would more likely be asked about the meeting before a conclusion is reached. These assumptions are usually exaggerated when carried from one person to the other spouse. This will be a test of trust and solidarity of the marriage and may require professional intervention to restore.

Fear and intimidation is another reason why many women abort their marriages. This is generally the result of repeated physical abuse by their husbands. Some women will try to tolerate this hostile environment through false promises and apologies from their husbands. Eventually the abuse will take its toll, and they will make the decision that enough is enough and terminate the marriage. By a large ratio men are the perpetuator of this abuse. There are many cases where women will impose their anger physically on their husband. "It is better to dwell in the corner of a house top than with a brawling woman in a wide house". Through their verbal attack, women will instigate physical altercation. There are many cases when either of the sexes will resort to violence to resolve their differences.

The church is a refuge that provides tremendous healing and resolution for some of these victims. Unfortunately many do not use the church or other outreach programs for counseling that will give them the confidence to restore trust in their spouse to try and restore their intimate relationship.

CHOICES, DECISIONS, & CONSEQUENCES

CHOICES, DECISIONS, & CONSEQUENCES

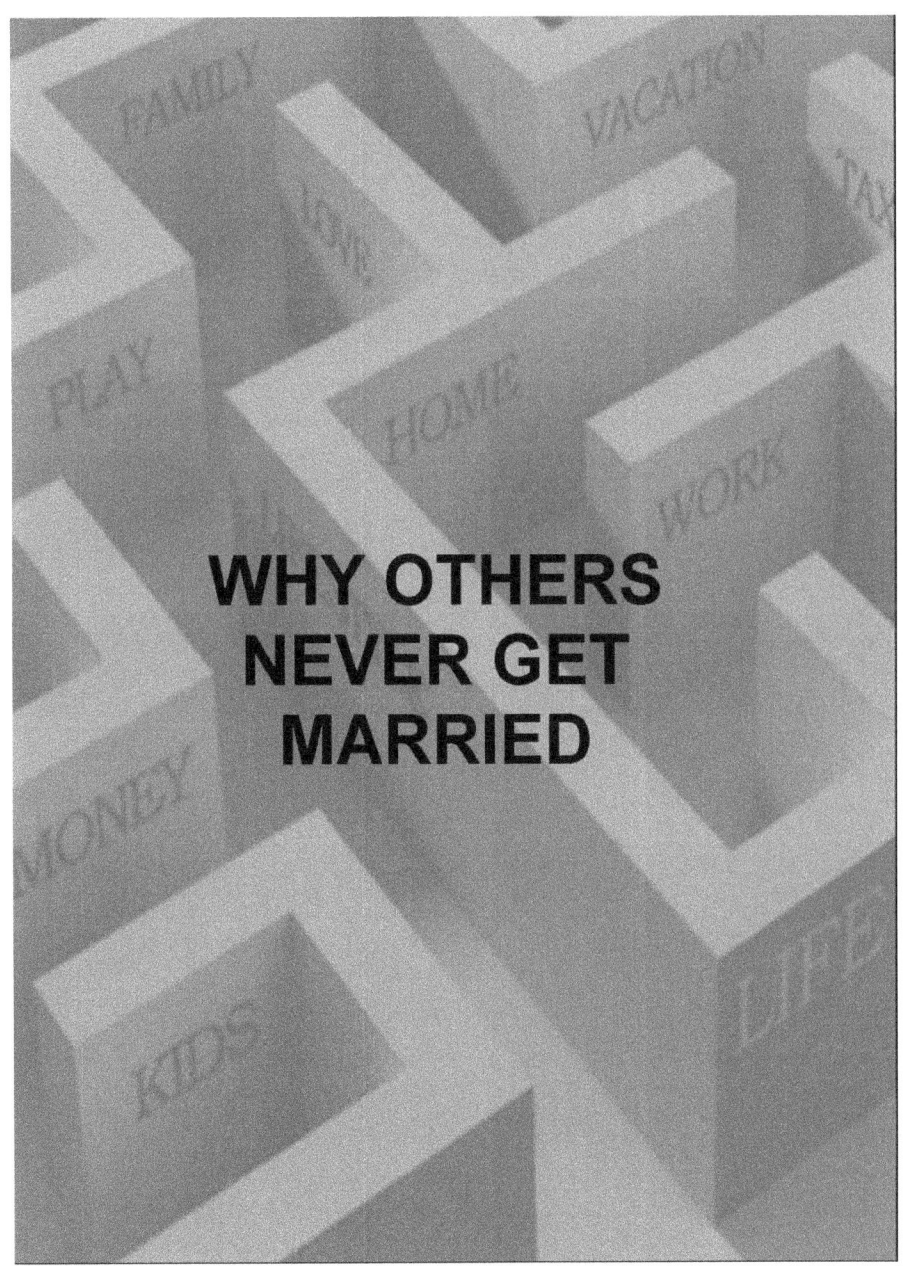

WHY OTHERS NEVER GET MARRIED

CHOICES, DECISIONS, & CONSEQUENCES

WHY OTHERS NEVER GET MARRIED

There is a large segment of our society who has made the choice never to get married. There are various reasons for this decision. If a person was involved in an intimate relationship before being married and experienced serious emotional hurt or physical abuse, then this bad experience will create a certain amount of fear and distrust for any long term intimate relationship. There will be reservation and reluctance to get involved in another intimate relationship for fear of repetition of those past negative experiences. Then the possibility of getting married would be very remote. These negative encounters sometimes leave permanent emotional scars, and all individuals of the opposite sex will be viewed in a stereotyped manner of continuing those unacceptable behaviors.

Sexual abuse at a young age by a family member or a trusted known adult will result in a withdrawal from any intimate long term relationship. This will not only limit the possibility of marriage but any intimate sexual relationship with the opposite sex. It is believed that the individual will enter into a rebellious state of mind and could resort to prostitution or homosexual behaviors.

There are many people who suffer from low self esteem, insecurity or an inferiority complex that affects their confidence level to be involved in a serious relationship with the opposite sex. They have a tendency of not being conversational at social functions, displaying a defensive posture to the opposite sex and sometimes getting the label "a loner". Many of these individuals make the decision to remain single. They view themselves as lacking the important qualities required to attract or satisfy a person of the opposite sex. With this mindset they will convince themselves that they are not worthy enough for marriage.

Then there is the playboy, who grows older but never matures. They usually have a very big ego and believed that they were created as God's gift to woman. They will convince themselves that they are entitled to sample as many women sexually as possible, without any permanent commitment. Their mindset is that it's all about them and will engage in this type of affair with women who will tolerate this type of relationship. Because of this irresponsible behavior many female hearts will be broken and will be left with illegitimate children without a father. When these men get older, they may not have any connection with these children and tend to have a lonely existence.

Others will give preference to their profession or job and view the permanence of marriage as a distraction and impeding their progress in their field of endeavor. They will be satisfied with a companion of the opposite sex, for social and sexual reasons with no intention for a long term commitment. God created man and woman to complement each other as wife and husband, and any decision to violate this concept is considered ungodly.

CHOICES, DECISIONS, & CONSEQUENCES

HOUSE OF WORSHIP

Along life's journey, we will eventually approach the mythical fork in the road where we will have to make a choice whether to change course to the spiritual walk or continue on the worldly path. This will be the most important lifestyle decision we will ever have to make. If our decision is to procrastinate on taking that spiritual walk until we determine that the right time should be when we have exhausted our worldly pleasures and activities, then it might be too late. Tomorrow is promised to no one, and we might die before our appointed time to make that transition to Christianity. If the decision is to dedicate the remainder of our life on a spiritual walk, then we must be prepared to terminate certain behaviors and habits that do not conform to the ways of the Lord. This will require us to choose a church where we will feel comfortable worshiping God.

The church is a house of worship that we should attend consistently to be refreshed spiritually and equipped mentally to resist the temptations that we encounter daily. When we are fed with the word constantly and are taught Godly principles and apply them to our daily lives, there will be a change in our priorities and behavior. We will be renewed spiritually and mentally with a different perspective of the secular world. Our friends and family will recognize our spiritual transformation and view us in a different light. "As we let our light shine, we unconsciously give other people permission to do the same" (Nelson Mandela). This would enable us to be a good role model for them to follow.

There should a desire to seek, find and attend a church regularly. A choice in your house of worship does not necessarily have to follow family tradition, race or status. This decision should be based on where the good word is preached and taught by a genuine Pastor where you will be fulfilled spiritually.

Growing up in my small rural town in Jamaica, there was a tendency to follow tradition in attending the same place of worship. The membership of my family's church consisted of various generational family groups. This was a means for families from various locations to come together and bond on a weekly basis while serving God.

Showing up in church does not give you a "present" check mark from God. We are not doing God a favor by attending church. Our only motive for going to church should be to seek redemption from our sinful deed, a time dedicated for reverence of the Lord, thanking and praising Him for granting us His grace and mercies.

To be consistently in a house of worship will enable us to receive His blessing that will propel us to a life of joy, happiness and prosperity. Being in this environment will reinforce the fact that "where two or three are gathered in my name there I am in the midst of them". The church is a place of refuge from this sinful world, and we should make the effort to be present as often as possible. "Those that choose to be planted in the house of The Lord shall flourish in his courts".

We should make a conscious decision to let go of the worldly pleasure and desire to embrace the church and its spiritual ideals. We will be fellowshipping with like minded Christians, where unity and love for all people are displayed and reinforced consistently.

It is important to be under the covering of a pastor that lives an exemplary Christian life that will allow his anointed blessings to flow down to his congregation. Being a pastor should not be a vocation but a call from God. There are many charismatic pastors that know the Bible, possess very good communicative skills, and have good influential powers, but do not live a life according to the word they preach. They will use the pulpit to satisfy their ego, acquire financial benefits, achieve celebrity status and exploit members for sexual fulfillment. When these behaviors become obvious, it will have a negative impact on church members.

They will become distrustful, uncomfortable and the Pastor will lose his credibility and some members may seek a new place of worship. When these deviant behaviors are revealed publicly, it gives ammunition to critics who will seize the opportunity to denounce and ridicule the Christian faith. Other churches with genuine spiritual leadership will be open to criticisms and stereotyping.

A good pastor will rebuke unchristian like behavior, regardless of the individual status or financial contribution to the church. Some pastors will give preferential treatment to members that contribute generously to the church for fear that they might leave and join another church. This concession could be an avenue for these individuals to exploit, manipulate and bribe the leadership within the church.

The divine and righteous objective of a pastor is to preach the word as he or she is inspired by God and not try to appease or satisfy the congregation with amusing and trivial sermons that will have a feel good effect. "Preach the word; be instant in season, out of season; reprove, rebuke, exhort with longsuffering and doctrine". If the sermons preached are spiritual and God fearing, the congregation should be focused and motivated by the messages and try to apply them to their daily lives.

There is no perfect church. The membership will be made up of the proverbial wheat and tares. The important thing is that there are more wheat than tares, and the tares will eventually be converted to wheat. There is no man or woman that is perfect and that includes the Pastor. As the spiritual leader, the Pastor's priority and emphasis should be a preacher and a teacher of the word. He should be dedicated to lead his flock to greener pastures, where there are still waters and showers of blessings. Under such leadership, the members will all be engaged, attentive and fulfilled with the word that will reinforce good Christian values. This will result in increased membership that will give greater credibility to his leadership and will enable an expansion of his territory to save more lost souls.

For a church to be fiscally successful, it will require cooperative and unified voluntary effort, from skilled personnel within its membership to perform administrative and manual tasks. My mother always tell us that "more hands make work light," and the more people participate for this cause will ease some of the financial expense of the church. There are operating expenses such utilities, rent/mortgage, maintenance and taxes that are an obligation to be fulfilled. Members should adhere to God's expectations of their tithing and offering to sustain and elevate the environment of their place of worship.

I am blessed to be a member of Hope International Church in Groveland Florida, where these principles and leadership qualities are always displayed. Our church serves as a spiritual melting pot, where the congregation is diverse in race, culture and nationality. Our Pastor Tony McCoy is a true example of what a preacher and teacher should be, by the Christian lifestyle he consistently exemplifies in his personal life and as our spiritual leader.

CHOICES, DECISIONS, & CONSEQUENCES

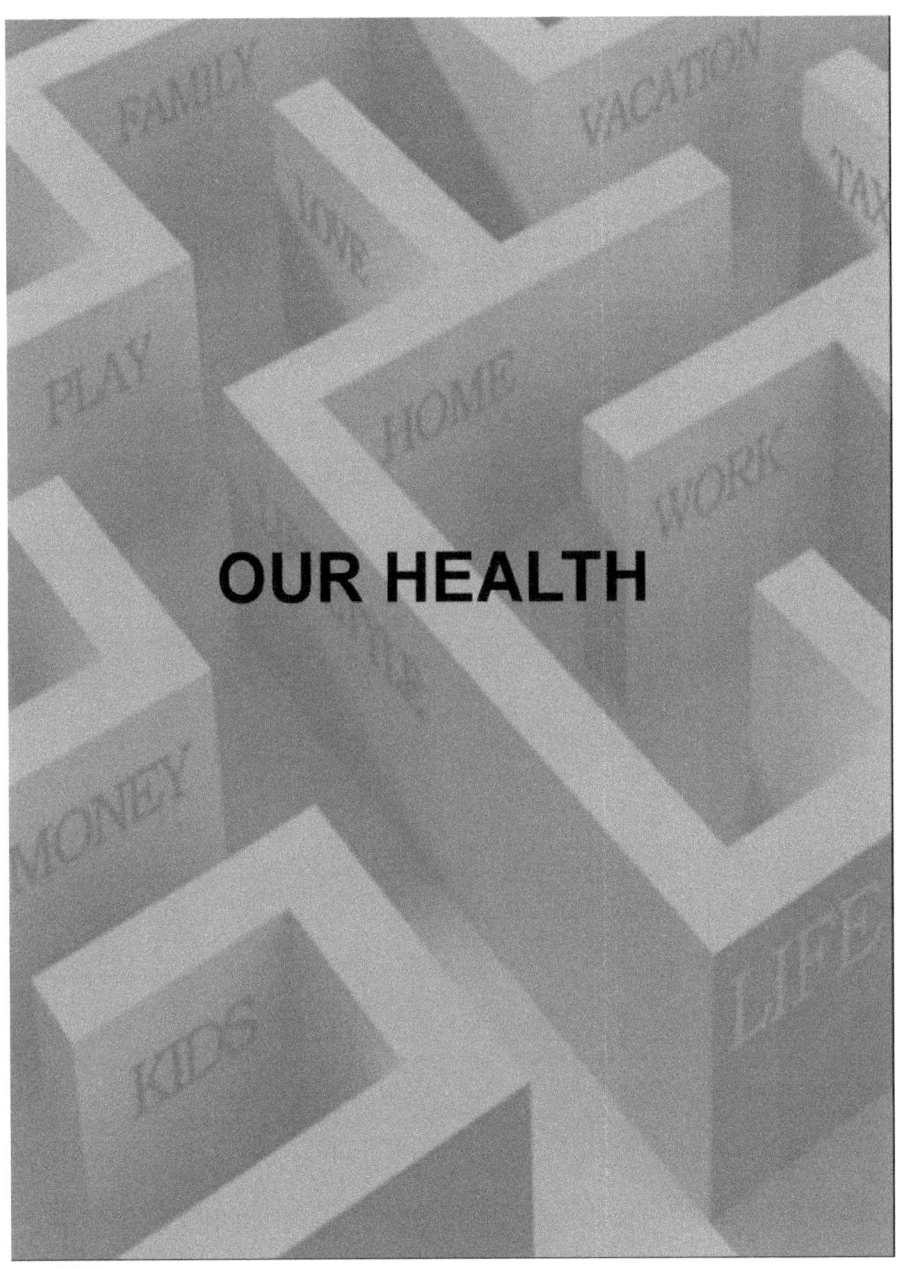

CHOICES, DECISIONS, & CONSEQUENCES

OUR HEALTH

Along life's journey, we should not be restricted from having fun that involves outdoor activities because of obesity and other medical issues. This would relegate us to be a spectator of the good times others are having. To be an active participant will require us to be physically, mentally and spiritually healthy. With these three principles active and in unison in our lives will enable us to be victorious, overcome all obstacles and the path of our life's journey will be clear and free from stress and disappointments.

We should make the decision to do all that is necessary to enjoy a good quality and healthy lifestyle. This can be attained by consistently having a nutritionally balanced diet, with regular exercise and adequate sleep at nights. There is no additional cost or effort for purchasing and preparing healthy ingredients for a nutritional meal. To make this decision would enhance our health, minimize the risk of terminal illness to our various organs and reduce the chance for obesity. We are prone to constantly indulge in meals that are satisfying and filling but are detrimental to our health. We constantly play Russian roulette with our lives, by eating what tastes good but is harmful to our bodies. We should try to give priority in eating what is good and nutritional that will be beneficial to our health.

Everything starts at home with our parents. If they consistently prepare nutritional diet for the family and monitor what their children eat at home, then this would serve as a template for the children to continue through adulthood. Today we see many young children that are obese, diabetic, have high blood pressure, or suffer from arthritis. These afflictions are generally related to the poor choice of food prepared by their parents. The availability of the numerous fast food establishments is very appealing to parents and children.

Today's children do not participate regularly in outdoor exercise activities that would restrict weight gain, improve their health and facilitate social interaction with their peers. They are addicted to indoor recreations, such as television, videos, the internet and all the recent electronic gadgets that are available to them. Playing these various indoor games robs them of an important aspect of growing up. While being entertained indoors, there will be an urge to munch on high cholesterol, low protein food and sodas that have negative health consequences.

Because many of today's parents are younger and indulge in these bad eating habits, then it serves as a confirmation to their children that this lifestyle is appropriate. The general excuses to justify bad eating habits are to blame it on family tradition. By continuing these unhealthy eating patterns of previous generation, we will continue the legacy of obesity and other negative health factors. There is a reluctance to change the habits that has been ingrained over the years. To break this traditional eating pattern will require a drastic mindset change. A conscious and disciplined effort has to be made to change to a proper nutritional diet that will ensure better health and quality of life. Many people have died prematurely, afflicted with various disease, are incapacitated from obesity, and poor blood circulation resulting from the effects of poor eating habits.

With the access of good health information via the internet, printed media and television, there is now more awareness of the consequences of these poor choices of diet. Obviously it is not what we know, it is what we do with the knowledge we have that will be beneficial to us.

An important criteria that will enable us to live longer is being optimistic and hopeful with great expectations when a health problem is diagnosed. Our mental attitude can influence the time and quality of our recovery. A positive state of mind, with the determination to overcome, will enable our body to resist and limit the impact of infection and various diseases that invades our body. A conceding or a "poor me" attitude will give permission for these illnesses to take control and destroy of our bodies. With a positive mindset and constant communication with the Lord through prayer will enable us overcome whatever ails us.

There are other indulgences that affect our health negatively. Abuse of alcohol, drugs, sex with numerous partners, and excessive nightlife activities contribute to ill health of varying degree and premature death. We have control over all these immoral conducts, but through peer pressure and lack of discipline we choose to engage in these behaviors.

With proper nutrition, and regular physical exercise, an annual medical checkup will not only ensure better health, but improve our physical outlook. A conscious decision should be made by women to monitor their breasts and men their prostate because these areas have a high rate of cancer.

It is very important that we incorporate personal development as a means of enriching our lives. This will entail reading 5-10 pages of intellectual book daily, listening to motivational CD's, associate with progressive people, and reduce the time allotted for watching television. These disciplinary acts will expand our knowledge, improve our vocabulary and give confidence in public speaking. The benefits will include improvements in our attitude, confidence and our ability to relate with people of a higher social and educational level. With this renewed inner self esteem we will step out boldly in life feeling secure and confident.

It is our choice to live a lifestyle that minimizes the risk of various health related issues by adhering to medical research recommendations on proper nutrition and exercise. A healthy state of mind is crucial in determining the right path along life's journey. This will enable us to improve on the quality of our lives and increase our lifespan.

CHOICES, DECISIONS, & CONSEQUENCES

CHOICES, DECISIONS, & CONSEQUENCES

DEBT

Debt is like a curse imposed on us for reckless and careless spending without any form of accountability. To be in debt is usually the result of bad choices in trying to acquire material things we cannot afford or trying to keep up with the "Joneses". Credit card spending is the main culprit that influences spontaneous and unnecessary spending, resulting in the accumulation of these debts. Banks and credit card companies make it easy and convenient to obtain a credit card through enticing promotions. We are inclined to spend much more with the convenience of a credit card than with cash.

We tend to ignore the consequences that these debts will have to be repaid. Credit card debts are penalized by high interest rates that make it harder to payoff. This puts us in an obligatory position to the lender to satisfy this debt at an agreed interest rate and monthly payment. We are like slaves to our various lenders and are robbed of recreational and social freedom because of these financial obligations.

Debt is not only from lending institution but friends, family, co-workers and employers. Great relationships are sometimes dissolved because of borrowing money and the inability to repay it by the agreed time. Employers may advance a portion of the salary to assist in an emergency situation. This will be deducted the next pay period which will result in a reduction in salary and create another crisis to satisfy other bills.

If we formulate a sound financial plan, with the discipline to incorporate savings, then we will be the lender and not the borrower. Being in debt is usually a self-imposed dilemma that can be remedied only through a change in our mindset. We should refocus our priorities to satisfy only our needs and limit recreational and clothing expenditures. Debt can cause serious stress, physical and mental pain, suicidal tendencies and in extreme cases murder of spouse or business partner.

Ignorance can be costly and making good decisions may require good counseling from a professional financial expert. We are inclined to believe that we want more money, but what we really need is the wisdom to properly allocate the money that we already have. There is a tendency to rely on our own intelligence and expertise that result in making bad financial decisions. The assumption that our income from our job, business and investment will continue forever gives us a false sense of security and result in the accumulation of debts.

To relieve ourselves from debt, we must decide on a change in our mindset that will change our attitude and decision making. This attitude adjustment will bring a consciousness to unnecessary spending and a desire to save more. We must renew our mind because as a man think, so is he. To achieve prosperity, you must first see yourself as being prosperous. We should aspire to achieve great wealth, and if we fall short and receive a portion, that would be better than not making the effort and receiving nothing.

Another analogy to realize prosperity is that we should not be contented with a cupful, or a bucketful but a barn full. For these goals to be realized we must have a reliable source of income and consistently apply good financial principles. The Good Lord does not want us to have a life of mediocrity but to have life abundantly. "But my God shall supply all my need according to his riches in glory by Christ Jesus".

A thought is like a seed in our subconscious, and when we consciously feed our minds with positive nutrients, we should expect to reap an abundant harvest. We will miss out on financial rewards if we do not plant seeds of faith on the fertile grounds of our minds and consistently nurture it to a prosperous fruition. With this renewal of our mind and change in attitude we will be motivated to make better decisions that will change our depressed financial circumstances. We should avoid envying the material and financial gains of others because we do not know what they went through to acquire them and what they are going through to keep them.

Financial bondage is being mentally controlled by the desire to have a lot of more money. "The love of money is the root of all evil" and can be considered a symbol of idolatry. By humility and fear of The Lord are riches and honor along life's journey. If we make good financial decisions we will spend our days in prosperity and our years in pleasure.

CHOICES, DECISIONS, & CONSEQUENCES

CHOICES, DECISIONS, & CONSEQUENCES

CHOICES, DECISIONS, & CONSEQUENCES

WEALTH

We have all had wishes and dreams of being exceedingly rich, enjoying a very opulent lifestyle but lack the commitment, the ambition, the ability or the know how to realize this dream. If being wealthy was easily attained then we all would live a life in wealth. It is believed that 5% of the people possess 95% of the wealth.

The two legitimate and ethical means of being wealthy are through inheritance or hard work with the discipline and commitment to fulfill the vision of an affluent lifestyle. Inherited wealth is a result of good financial decisions by a predecessor that is generally handed down to family members. It is usually the result of wise investment, good money management and the discipline to satisfy their needs, not wants.

People of great wealth have a tendency to have a philanthropist mindset by donating money to educational and medical institutes, giving to the poor, tithing and offering to their church. These acts of generosity are Godly principles which will be rewarded with continued increase and sustenance of their wealth. If the inheritor continues those principles and values, then this wealth will benefit the next generation.

The acquisition of wealth through hard work will require proper education, training and competent personnel in their business venture. Being an entrepreneur is the creation of a small business that drives the economy of most countries. This is an avenue that aggressive, business minded people venture into for the purpose of financial success. With the right business model, at the right location and good marketing, some small business have the potential to become major corporations.

CHOICES, DECISIONS, & CONSEQUENCES

When properly organized and managed, with the commitment to persevere over all obstacles, this business venture has rewarded many with tremendous wealth. Many people have invested time and money in these ventures but give up at the first sign of economical downturn and become victims of the prevailing circumstances before realizing their ultimate goal.

There are many among us hoping that our six numbers from the lotto will eventually be a winner to bring us instant wealth. The odds of realizing this lotto windfall is very remote. People continue to pour out lots of money into this method of gambling, wishing on a star that their time to reap this big reward will eventually come. "Wealth gotten by vanity will diminish; but he that gathereth by labor shall increase". If the money is not earned through hard work and sacrifices, it will not be appreciated and spent recklessly until it is all gone.

To retain and increase wealth will require discipline, consistency, perseverance and a designated financial goal. In the pursuit of acquiring wealth will be many obstacles to overcome along this journey. We will fall many times in this pursuit, but it will be our ability to rise more determined after each fall, that will enable us to overcome those obstacles that may impede our progress. For a positive and successful result we should always put God first, align ourselves with successful people, attend financial seminars and incorporate various methods of saving.

To be the best, we must learn from the best. A decision should be made to be in the company and environment of successful people. "We have not because we ask not" and the principle of associating with successful people, we should always be asking questions and applying their answers and recommendations to our business venture. Hearing and knowing good principles will not ensure success, but by applying that knowledge effectively and consistently will enhance our chances for success.

There are many obvious advantages to being wealthy. The ability to send our children to the best schools, live in the most desirable neighborhood, drive expensive cars and vacation in the most exotic places. Wealth gives us comfort and status but is not the recipe for true happiness. The main ingredients for happiness are peace of mind, a healthy self esteem, good health, spiritual fortitude, and contentment from a happy marriage with a wholesome family. There are many wealthy people that experience depression, loneliness and being miserable that their money cannot satisfy.

Some wealthy folks, because of their egos, will socialize with the elite crowd and engage in big spending to impress and gain acceptance. These conducts usually come at a steep cost and are the reason for depleting huge portions of financial resources that took years to acquire. Prosperity is viewed as a result of financial gains and by the outward appearance of their accomplishment. If the effort is not made to be thrifty and monitor expenditures, then this wealth could be eroded.

Prosperity acquired without acknowledging God's blessings and not being generous cannot withstand lengthy depressed economic periods. Only divine prosperity that is ordained by God because of our spiritual lifestyle can out perform economical turbulences. Divine prosperity is immune to volatile economic cycles and will endure for a lifetime. We should not lose sight of the fact that everything we acquire belongs to God and we are entrusted to be good stewards of his money and possessions. "Both riches and honor comes from Thee and Thou reign over all". The best investment that will ensure continued success and retain our wealth is to be obedient to Godly principles of tithing and being generous to those that are in need.

CHOICES, DECISIONS, & CONSEQUENCES

CHOICES, DECISIONS, & CONSEQUENCES

CHOICES, DECISIONS, & CONSEQUENCES

RETIREMENT

This is the period along life's journey where we are supposed to enjoy the fruits of our youthful labor, with the ability to choose what form of activity to engage in that will bring the most fun and satisfaction. The best and most productive years of our lives will be spent in the workforce. The main objectives are to try to achieve financial reward for our hard work that will enable us to enjoy a good quality retirement lifestyle.

During our working years we continue to speak and envision a retirement of peace and prosperity. To achieve the ideal retirement would require us to make good financial decisions, with the discipline to adhere to a well formulated saving plan without interruption and minimize withdrawal. Other criteria for success would be consistency and longevity of employment, planting productive financial seeds with the right institutions and nurturing them to a successful harvest. Executing these plans and behavior will provide us with the financial resources to enjoy our choice in recreational activities, vacation to places we find appealing and participating in family activities.

It is imperative that we maintain a strong family connection, spend quality time with children and grandchildren. For us to be able to indulge in all these recreational activities will require us to be good health. It is very important that we exercise consistently, maintain a healthy nutritional diet and regular medical examination.

We should dedicate time to worship and thank God for sparing our lives to be able to live to the age of retirement. Going to church regularly, living a Godly life, and fellowshipping with people of like minds will complete our state of being. We will have the time to volunteer service for various organizations helping the poor and needy. This goodwill gesture will enable us to interact socially and help to improve the lives of others at the same time. Giving back generously of our time and money to society will reward us with God's blessing.

Age does not dictate retirement now as it did previously. Early retirement can be realized from inheritance, a comprehensive retirement plan, good investments that produces solid returns, an insurance windfall and above average income from your profession. There are early retirements as a result of poor health or an accident that inhibits movements. Depending on the severity of these situations, retirement will have its limitation in physical and recreational enjoyment.

There are people who make poor choices during their working years. No stability in employment, poor financial choices, reckless spending and negative family issues will hamper their chances of a good financial reserve to enjoy their retirement. Others may see their retirement reserve depleted because of major decline in the stock market. In many of these cases, their only source of consistent reliable income is from Social Security. This will require a very serious adjustment in lifestyle, because social security returns may not be enough to maintain a decent living. Because of this dilemma many are forced to make the decision of returning to work.

To return to the workforce in your senior years for financial reasons can be very challenging. Seniors may encounter age discrimination and may be subjected to a lower salary for the position. They will be competing with younger, more aggressive applicants that will be viewed as better long term investments by most companies. Many companies are reluctant to hire seniors because they are not as productive, and they present a liability with regards to health issues.

I retired from my job as an inspector for the construction of roads and bridges. Being very active and vibrant, I did not intend to retire in the typical recreational and relaxed lifestyle. I decided to start a new career as a real estate agent. A declining economy and the devaluation of property directly affected the Real Estate market that impacted my finances negatively. This presented an opportunity for me to be resourceful to explore other avenues for a source of income. God works in a mysterious way. Through His Divine intervention I was motivated to be an author. I now realize that I have a hidden talent to write and I will unleash my full potential to be the best at this new career.

Many retirees seek employment for the purpose of interacting with people, to remain physically active and mentally alert. Because this is not for financial reward, their choices of employment are usually at establishments where the duties are less laborious with minimal mental stress.

A successful retirement would be one where there is stability in your finances, health, family relationship and a Godly lifestyle. To be blessed in all these areas would enable us to have peace and tranquility where our latter years would be our better years.

CHOICES, DECISIONS, & CONSEQUENCES

CHOICES, DECISIONS, & CONSEQUENCES

WE SHOULD ENJOY OUR LIFE

God gave us the gift of life that he wants us live enjoyably, productively and abundantly in love and harmony with our fellow man. To maintain this lifestyle we should make the effort daily to read and abide by life instructional manual the Holy Bible. In so doing there will be a high probability that the rest of our years will be the best of our years.

We should try to do the right things spiritually, emotionally and physically now that will bring us joy and happiness later. To be truly happy, we must first love ourselves as God loves us. He will never leave us or forsake us in spite of our sinful and rebellious ways. He wants us to be the victor and not the victim in our pursuit for happiness.

To realize a fulfilled and enjoyable life will require the implementation and execution of a happy state of mind. We should try to be in the company of positive, fun-loving people. This is a good prescription for a happy state of mind. We will never be elevated to a higher altitude if we do not adjust our negative attitude. There should be a freedom in our mind with clarity of thoughts to appreciate, recognized and live in harmony on God's perfectly created earth. With these qualities within, success will abound in our lives.

There should be a freedom of fear, worry and mood swings that have a tendency of casting negative spell on our lives. We should not allow worry to rob us of these important aspects of our lives. Worrying is a complete waste of our time and does not solve any problem. To worry is self inflicted torture with disturbing thoughts that can result in a state of depression, affect our attitude, and impact our health negatively. Sometimes we worry because we are disappointed when we are unable to solve our problem. But if we "trust in the Lord with all our heart: and lean not unto our own understanding" then there would be no reason to worry.

Fear is another culprit that steals our joy. "For God hath not given us the spirit of fear; but of power, and of love, and of a sound mind". Faith and fear cannot inhabit our state of mind at the same time. If we allow fear to gain control, then we will deny ourselves of enjoying life to the fullest. We need to step out boldly with faith and the assurance that with God at our side we will be victorious over all circumstances. There is a fear of success because this would elevate us to a level beyond friends and family that we will be reluctant to leave behind. There is the fear of failure because of lack the inner confidence, low self esteem and insecurity that will restrict us to a life of mediocrity. We should replace fear with faith in God, that he will walk with us and direct our path through turbulence and unforeseen dangers.

We should try to develop emotional stability that will prevent mood swing from interfering with our ability to better interact with our fellow man. Our physical mood swings affect our mental state of mind that results in withdrawal, isolation and antisocial behaviors. These unpredictable reactions from being up one day and down the next can ruin relationships with friends and family. They will never know what to expect because of the inconsistency in our behavioral pattern. We need stability in our emotions daily and stop wasting time in self pity.

In evaluating ourselves we have the tendency to focus on our faults and ignore the many positive qualities we possess. We should resist the temptation of demeaning ourselves and focus on complementing and lifting ourselves up to the highest level where God wants us to be. We should make a conscious decision to enjoy every minute of every day regardless of the circumstances or crises we are experiencing.

It is God's will that we have a life of prosperity and not a life in poverty or being depressed. Life is too short to allow our circumstances to rob us of our joy. Whatever we see or experienced is temporary and is in transition. God works in the spiritual realm which we cannot see, but with faith, patience and obedience He will deliver us in His appointed time with the relief we need. He is an on time God and His time is always the right time when He will eliminate all our problems and hardship and replace them with peace and happiness. Only He can satisfy the desires of our heart that will bring joy and happiness to our lives.

It is very important that we try to live in the now. Time is precious and we should endeavor to accomplish positive results with our efforts now. Sometimes we do not appreciate the good things we have accomplished by chasing after perceived treasures beyond our reach. We should not postpone having a good time until we acquire a prescribe amount of money to satisfy our need to be happy at some later date. Money does not buy happiness. Happiness has to come from within, with a positive mindset and the motivation to put aside all distractions that may interfere with the good times we should be having now.

Happiness begins at home. Coming from a happy home environment will be displayed in our daily activities and will impact the people we associate with positively. Enjoyment can be with family or friends participating in a variety of recreational activities that everyone can engage in for fun and laughter. Enjoyment does not have to be only recreational but anything that brings fulfillment, stress relief, peace and satisfaction to us.

Peace is a gift given to us through Christ Jesus that we all have access to and it should be fully utilized. True peace is realized when there is a Godly state of mind resulting from a healthy relationship with God. Peace can be synonymous with happiness which we are all entitled to enjoy.

Along life's journey we will have to interact with different people and our attitude towards them can determine their response that can affect our happiness. To have total enjoyment and a fulfilled life we must make the effort to treat people the way we want to be treated. We should always show love, compassion, friendliness and forgiveness to others, and these acts will be returned to us. We should express appreciation and gratitude when we are the recipient of kindness from others. We should try resolving all differences in a civil and peaceful manner void of arguments and malice. Most of all it is imperative to have a healthy relationship with God and constantly express thanks and gratitude for the ability to enjoy our life.

CHOICES, DECISIONS, & CONSEQUENCES

About the Author: Rudolph Burke

Rudolph Burke is the CEO, of Trinity Professional Services Inc. He is an author, and an entrepreneur. Rudolph Burke has worked with several of the large Real Estate brokerage firms in Orlando, Florida.

Rudolph Burke has the desire to leave a legacy for his children's children. He has the heart to serve others throughout his community, and is an inspiring wealth builder.

As an author, Rudolph's purpose is to inspire and motivate readers to have a closer relationship with God that will enhance all aspects of their lives.

His expectation is to achieve the highest distinction and recognition as an author who transformed the lives of readers both positively and spiritually.

CHOICES, DECISIONS, & CONSEQUENCES

Notes

Notes

Notes

Notes